KU-278-519

Raising Spirits

Allotments, well-being and community

Jenny Mollison,
Judy Wilkinson and
Rona Wilkinson

ARGYLL ✦ PUBLISHING

First published by Argyll Publishing in 2014.

Registered Office 1 Rutland Court, Edinburgh

© Jenny Mollison, Judy Wilkinson and Rona Wilkinson

The moral rights of the authors have been asserted.

A catalogue record of this book is available from the British Library

ISBN 978-1-908931-59-7

This book is sold subject to the condition that it shall not by way of trade or otherwise, be lent, resold, hired out or otherwise circulated without the publisher's prior consent in any form of binding or cover other than that in which it is published and without a similar condition including this condition imposed on the subsequent purchaser. All rights reserved. No part of this publication may be reproduced, stored in a retrieval system or transmitted in any form or by any means, electronic, mechanical or otherwise without the written permission of the publisher.

Dundee & Angus College Library
Gardyne Campus

Accession Barcode...006884.....

Class Number...306 MOL.........

Date Added......19/5/15.............

Contents

Acknowledgements

We would like to thank all the plotholders across Scotland who have contributed stories, laughter and valuable insights.

Foreword

People are attracted to allotments for many different reasons, whether it's an escape from the stresses of the world, or a reversion back to nature. It often represents a sort of backlash against the trappings of the modern world, and the need to keep hold of a tradition that has to increasingly fight for its relevance in a society populated by plentiful access to food from cheaper and easier sources.

This is one of the quotations from an exhibition on the Heritage of Glasgow Allotments and I agree wholeheartedly with the sentiments.[1] Indeed I believe that allotments have the potential not just to keep our feet on the ground but to help maintain our sanity in a society which increasingly appears to be going off the rails.

This is why this book on allotments is such an important addition to the *Postcards from Scotland* series for which I am Commissioning Editor. The series is designed to outline some of the main social, economic, environmental and cultural challenges of our times as well as to encourage new ways of thinking and living.

In the first book, *After Now* (2012), public health experts Phil Hanlon and Sandra Carlisle outline some of the 'dis-eases' of modernity such as the epidemic of obesity and problematic drug and alcohol use from which Scotland particularly suffers.[2] They argue that materialism, consumerism and individualism are some of the root causes of contemporary problems and I take up this theme in the second book of the series – *The Great Takeover: How materialism, the media and markets now dominate our lives* (2012).[3] In it I draw on copious empirical research to show that the more people pursue materialist values in life (money, image and popularity) the worse their well-being is likely to be.

If all this sounds negative and pessimistic, fear not as the series is not just interested in analysing problems: it also aims to highlight how so many people in Scotland are not only aware of these types of issues but are already taking steps to change their lives or at least adopt a different set of values.

The third book in the series is by Alf and Ewan Young and it's called *The New Road* (2012).[4] It's the story of a father and son's eight day journey round fifteen inspirational projects in Scotland. One of these projects is the Fife Diet run by Mike Small and he picks up the baton for the fourth book entitled *Scotland's Local Food Revolution* (2013).[5] This book combines trenchant analysis of a 'dysfunctional' food system with an upbeat outline of all the great things which are happening in Scotland to support local food.

Allotments feature in *The New Road* as some of the projects Alf and Ewan visited included plots or community gardens and, inevitably, Mike Small returns to the topic as they are an integral part of the local food revolution he describes.

The fifth book in the series is called *Letting Go: Breathing new life into organisations* (2013) by Tony Miller and

Gordon Hall.[6] At first glance this topic seems to have nothing to do with the type of issues raised in this book but this isn't the case. One of the authors' main pleas in *Letting Go* is for managers and organisations to move away from the stultifying conformity of contemporary work with its targets, tick-boxes and performance management and allow much more room for individual judgement and creativity.

What is missing from the contemporary workplace was once so evident in traditional allotments. According to Jenny Mollison, Judy Wilkinson and Rona Wilkinson, the authors of this book, allotment sites were traditionally able to offer plotholders an opportunity for creativity and healthy individuality through, for example, the design of their huts and other features. Sadly this is no longer the case in some contemporary sites because of the modern obsession with standardisation.

Nonetheless, as the three show so well in their first chapter, allotments have a substantial contribution to make to individual well-being, community cohesion and so many other aspects of modern life that we could talk about allotments providing us with a veritable cornucopia of benefits.

The book also takes us through a brief history of allotments, basic issues of design and access, governance options, what's happening in other countries, new types of produce being grown and more innovative ways for plotholders to work with the elements.

As Commissioning Editor for the series I always wanted the books to be, in modern parlance, 'embodied' – i.e. reflecting real, lived experience rather than the abstract ideas of a solitary writer divorced from the world. And you don't get much more down to earth or gritty than *Raising Spirits*. As you read the book you can almost hear the shovel breaking the soil, smell the herbs, taste the tomatoes and see butterflies fluttering from leaf to leaf.

The series is also designed to get people to think about values; to realise that the materialist values we are encouraged to pursue at every turn are not good for our well-being and to pursue values which are more fulfilling and attainable. Yet again this book has these positive, 'pro-social', pro well-being values in, quite literally, spades. This book helps us to see that plotholders are not only digging their allotments and planting seeds but are also cultivating values: thrift; respect for nature and biological limits; friendship; community; simplicity and so much more. Plotholders are also learning the valuable skills of food production which no resilient community can afford to ignore.

In short as plotholders go about their allotment sites they are not only cultivating produce for themselves and their families: they are demonstrating the very values which many more people need to embrace if we are to create a more sustainable, healthy and fulfilling way of life.

CHAPTER ONE
An abundance of benefits

> When highly stressed people are asked to visualize
> a soothing scene, nobody imagines a freeway or
> shopping mall. Rather, images of wilderness, forest,
> seascape, and starry skies invariably emerge.

So wrote Theodore Roszak, the man who first coined the
term 'ecopsychology' and who was ahead of his time in
arguing for the importance of nature to people's health and
well-being.[7] In the last decade various psychologists and
thinkers have followed suit arguing that contact with the
green world is imperative for people's well-being. Indeed
bestselling author Richard Louv talks about 'nature-deficit
disorder'.[8] Numerous empirical research projects have
supported the idea that contact with nature is good for
people's health. For example, when subjects in experiments
are shown pleasant natural scenes they are then more likely
to engage in health promoting behaviours.[9] Other research
studies have shown that those living in green environments
are less likely to be aggressive.[10] Researchers have also shown
that walking in a green environment, as opposed to an urban
area, can improve attention and memory as well as calming
and improving mood. This is why professionals now talk
about 'green therapy'.[11]

Nature truly has the capacity to soothe and make us feel better by having a 'restorative' effect.[12] So too can quiet spaces. Some people report wanting to escape from their increasingly crowded and stressful lifestyles into a quiet place to reconnect with their 'inner selves'. Big companies including Apple, Google, Deutsche Bank, Proctor and Gamble and Nike now offer meditation or relaxation spaces in their headquarters and workplaces. Some people have meditation spaces in their houses or gardens. We know from experience that allotment plots offer a place that an individual can use for quiet contemplation. Plotholders can sit in the sun or even practise yoga or mindfulness as well as cultivate the land. Some folk even say that weeding is a form of meditation (although children in the family may disagree).

In her Merlin Trust report (2001), entitled 'To all the Ingenious Allotment Gardeners of Scotland', the environmentalist Caitlin DeSilvey writes:

> . . . at the Perth allotments, I met a woman with a
> glorious honeysuckle bower gracing the entrance to
> her flower-full allotment. Barbel Roerig's garden is
> a place for sitting and thinking as much as for
> hoeing and harvesting, with benches tucked behind
> banks of berries and a hut with an oven and a
> sewing machine. The Perth allotments, on
> Moncrieffe Island in the River Tay, can be reached
> only by a narrow footbridge along the railway. Many
> of the gardeners at the site use their plots as a
> retreat, and perhaps because of this flowers
> abounded, roses and fuchsias, delphinium and
> poppies, dahlias and Livingstone daisies.[13]

Allotments not only offer stress release and regular access to green and quiet space but have other health benefits as well. Richard Mitchell is Professor of Health and Environment at the University of Glasgow and he points out that 'proximity to quality green space doesn't only make you feel better, it actually makes you better! Blood pressure, hormones, and stress all respond favourably'.[14]

When we put on top of this the physical exercise allotments demand then we can see how the health benefits of working a plot are as profuse as many of the wild flowers that grow there. Jenny Mollison, one of this book's co-authors, explained the health benefits of allotments in one of her *Scotsman* articles:

> Most of what I do when I am gardening involves the kind of exercise which some of my friends pay for at a gym. I indulge in plenty of bending and stretching as I weed and prune. There's some weight-training as I hump sacks of compost around, and finally, there's some aerobic exercise as I dig. And I do this in fresh air to the accompaniment of all the glorious sounds and smells of the great outdoors.[15]

Huts provide the opportunity for all the year round activity. They are meeting places even in winter for neighbourhood gossip with tea and the occasional fry-up. A bonfire on a crisp autumn day can be a real pleasure as well as fulfilling other needs. A carefully laid fire on the ground or in a galvanised bin is a good way of disposing of waste which cannot be composted. Spent potato haulms, raspberry canes and old, dry strawberry foliage are examples of materials which might harbour disease or are too woody for composting. A bonus is dining out on potatoes baked in the embers.

All of these end of year tasks contribute to a healthy lifestyle.

Well-being

Well-being is not just the absence of pain, discomfort and incapacity. It is a positive physical, social and mental state. There are lots of different ways to define well-being and to discuss its characteristics but we favour the definition of well-being which stresses the importance of an individual's personal goals, skills and creativity as well as relationships and community.[16] An allotment site literally provides a space for these different strands of well-being to come together. Let's first look at individual development.

We live in an increasingly homogenised world where people can become slaves to fashion and trying to achieve the 'right' look. Allotments, however, provide plotholders with a great opportunity to develop and display their creativity and individuality. For example, there are some wonderful huts made of recycled materials with lace curtains, doors with brass knockers, Charles Rennie Mackintosh windows and old calor gas cylinders refashioned as wood stoves. Recycled windows can be used to create glasshouses where even more exotic plants and fruit can be grown. Even recycled bathtubs can become a 'garden feature'. Thrift and recycling easily go hand in hand with creativity. Allotments have long been the last resting place for a miscellany of odds and ends no longer needed for their original purpose. Transparent roof sheets from a redundant carport make wonderful cloches and old sash windows make the ultimate cold frames. Floorboards are good for edging beds and old bus shelters make sturdy glasshouses. All of these started with an idea and tell us something about the plotholder.

Even without these types of features, allotment plots are

an expression of the individual's personality: the neat and tidy can delight in rows of perfect vegetables, all in line; those of a wilder disposition have mixed beds, companion planting and flowers; and those with an artistic bent may have beans or sweet peas growing over arches, small rock gardens and ponds or large ornamental cardoons, which are good to eat and show.

Food

Then there is the food – local food, seasonal food, food you have grown yourself. Good gardeners can provide most of the vegetables and fruit for their families which are both organic and seasonal. Neighbours swap recipes and stories. New plotholders are often amazed at how produce direct from the plot tastes so much better. Nowadays with green-houses, cold frames and special seeds almost all fruit and vegetables can be produced at some time of the year. Some plotholders have always managed peaches, figs and grapes but now we can find peppers, aubergines, and even kumquats. Growing your own brings the excitement back into food.

During the summer months, seasonal gluts are common when, for example, the supply of courgettes and beans exceeds demand. On these occasions, plotholders share the bounty with their friends or donate it to their site's open days. Others will make arrangements with local organisa-tions, including soup kitchens, day care centres and schools who are always grateful for donations of this kind.

Some experienced growers compiled the Musselburgh Allotments' Cookery Book to enable plotholders to make the most imaginative use of their seasonal gluts.[17] As a result of a newspaper article, demand for this book ran into thousands as requests from home and abroad came in.

We all know that for a variety of health reasons everyone should be eating a minimum of five portions of fruit and vegetables a day. However, it is estimated that less than a third of people in the UK comply. The figure for Scotland is significantly lower with less than a fifth (19 per cent) of Scots eating the recommended number of fruit and vegetables. Some experts believe that this may partially account for Scotland's poor health record. What's worrying is that despite the publicity for the importance of healthy eating, fruit and vegetable consumption in Scotland has not increased since 2003.[18]

Given the importance of this issue, and the fact that allotments and community gardens could help boost some Scots' intake of fruit and vegetables, we are delighted that health boards are now playing a part in promoting community gardens and allotments. For example, in 2012 NHS Greater Glasgow and Clyde became involved in a project called SAGE (Sow and Grow Everywhere) at Gartnavel Hospital. The site now includes spaces for community gardens where staff, patients and visitors can grow vegetables, herbs and flowers. One of the main purposes of the project is to get people eating more locally produced seasonal produce.[19]

One of the skills that has been lost over the years is the ability to cook fresh vegetables. This is being addressed by several community organisations that either have their own community gardens or plots on allotment sites and offer cookery classes. For example, the North Glasgow Community Food Initiative has plots on three allotment sites and it –

... hopes to strengthen community knowledge and individual skills about the importance of healthy eating and subsequent impacts on healthy living practices. We also see cookery as a medium for encouraging cross-cultural understanding and facilitating the exchange of cultural experiences. We have run several cookery classes each year including a men's cookery group, international cookery exchange groups and youth cookery skills groups. We have had people from all ages, cultures and languages attend our sessions.[20]

The benefits are particularly evident for children. It is commonplace these days to hear about how children are so alienated from the land and countryside that they don't know, for example, where milk, eggs or meat come from. However, one story we heard recently particularly troubled us. A primary school teacher in Ayrshire asked her class of twenty plus pupils to bring in a potato the next day for a printing project. Only three obliged. Some had forgotten to ask but a good number said that their parents didn't have potatoes at home as they didn't buy them. She found out that they were only eating processed potato products such as chips. And this is in Ayrshire! – the home of what many consider to be the best Scottish potatoes.

So allotments and community gardens can help children to understand where vegetables come from. Andy Forrester is involved with children at Playbusters in the east end of Glasgow and they have an 'intergenerational' plot on West-thorn allotments. He tells us, 'Before the allotment plot the kids thought carrots came from ASDA, now they can't wait to wash and eat their own.'

Meeting grounds of hearts and minds

These days building a community and getting to know your neighbours is more difficult than it used to be with changing work patterns, extensive use of private cars and much more in-home entertainment such as television viewing. Solo living is rising steeply. Families are also getting smaller and regular interaction with extended family less common than it used to be. All this means that there has been a large rise in the number of people who describe themselves as 'lonely'. This is no small matter as human beings are social animals and need the company of others to feel happy and healthy. Indeed one research report recently claimed that in today's society loneliness is now a bigger killer than obesity.[21]

Yet again allotments have a great contribution to make to this social problem as they facilitate interaction and community. Allotment sites provide a space where the plotholders meet on a regular informal basis and just talk. They are often like traditional village streets where neighbours have to walk past each other and share trials and tribulations such as weather, slugs, and pigeons. Differences disappear over discussions of different vegetables, how to deal with pests or the antics of the resident fox.

Allotment sites provide a meeting ground where people work together and learn to understand others' strengths and vulnerability. On many sites there are community huts with, if you are lucky, facilities for tea, a place to sit and chat and where gardening magazines, information, spare seeds and plants can all be left for other plotholders. There have always been social activities on sites. Throughout the 1920s and 30s dances took place after the summer shows. Today barbecues,

Halloween parties and open days have taken their place but still bring people together to celebrate 'growing'. In Musselburgh, after many years of allotment gardening, Jack and Ruth Suffolk felt so much at home with their fellow plotholders that it seemed natural to them to celebrate their golden wedding anniversary amongst those people with whom they had spent so many happy gardening years.

Paul is a good example of someone whose life has been transformed through his involvement with an allotment site. Here's how one of his friends describes his transformation:

> Paul isn't a very confident gardener but he can turn any old bit of wood into something wonderful and is quick to offer his help to others when they are building or repairing huts, fences, greenhouses or doing other jobs on the plot. The fact that he owns a very sturdy trailer also adds to his list of good points on the plot and he is regularly off out with other plotholders foraging for slabs, timber, logs or compost, anything that is going to waste but is highly desirable to us scavengers for a new life on the plot.

> Last year his plot was bursting at the seams with produce, full for the first time in his six years there, and Paul was over the moon and gaining confidence in his gardening skills as he tended and harvested his crops.

> One particularly lovely summer evening I was having a cup of tea with Paul's wife, Liz. She isn't a regular visitor to the plot and she was amazed to see how it was blossoming under Paul's care. As we chatted Liz revealed that in over 35 years of marriage this was the first time she could recall that Paul had ever had more than one friend that he

> talked about and he genuinely looked forward to
> coming to the plot and was always talking about
> who he was meeting up with and what plans they
> were making. 'It's the best thing that's ever
> happened to him,' she said.

Members of the Simon Community have tended a plot in Oatlands Leisure Gardens for many years but community groups taking plots on allotment sites is a growing trend. This means that group members become part of the allotment community. The 2007 Audit of Scotland's Allotments found that there were over 50 different local community groups involved with sites and that this number had burgeoned in the previous year.[22] On Hamiltonhill in Glasgow, for example, there are plots for the North Glasgow Food Initiative, EMMAUS, the Unison Women's Group, and the Hamilton Learning Centre. There are also three local primary schools attending weekly classes on growing fruit and vegetables as well as learning about wildlife. All this provides a chance for people from many different walks of life to come together on a shared task.

Mental health

Allotments can make a contribution towards preventing the onset of mental health illnesses.

In 2007 Juliet Johnson undertook research as part of her degree in Occupational Therapy. In her dissertation entitled 'How does taking part in a community allotment group affect the everyday lives, self perception and social inclusion of participants?' she writes:

> People with mental health problems are amongst
> the most socially excluded in society. Horticultural
> therapy has been shown to have positive outcomes,
> with projects on allotment sites also promoting
> social inclusion with other plotholders, using the
> common interest of gardening.[23]

Her research showed that the psychosocial benefits of allotment groups are further enhanced by participation in projects involving a diverse group of volunteers. She also demonstrated that volunteering was both inclusive and de-stigmatising, with participants widening social networks, being valued by the community and escaping 'sick-role' identity. Meaning and purpose in taking part in gardening with other like-minded people increased a sense of meaning and purpose in participants' lives.

Philip, a plotholder at Kinnaird allotments corroborated this finding. He reports that his plot is his 'bit of Scotland' and that allotments are a personal therapeutic garden which helped him fight depression:

> Jam made from my raspberries gives a meaning to
> life. Living in a tower block is like living in a
> hencoop and on my plot I have my own space
> where I can get away from it all and switch off or, if
> I feel like company there are people from different
> countries and different backgrounds to talk to.[24]

The contribution which gardening can make to the recovery of those suffering from mental health illnesses has long been recognised. Throughout the country there are old hospitals with large areas of garden ground and sometimes orchards. In the past these served the dual purpose of providing fresh food for the hospital together with meaningful activity for the patients.

Trellis is the Scottish charity specialising in therapeutic gardening. It supports a network of over 200 therapeutic gardening projects in Scotland, including some in secure units. They justifiably pride themselves on using gardening to help people take care of their physical, emotional and social well-being. Their reports and case studies of successful therapeutic gardening contribute to the wealth of evidence of a link between increased well-being and gardening.

The new Forth Valley Royal Hospital is set in extensive grounds which, until 2002, were home to the Royal Scottish National Hospital, a state mental hospital with a walled garden as well as loch and woodland areas. The Royal Edinburgh Hospital's garden and orchard are being redeveloped for community gardens. Amongst their activities is a gardening group supporting the hospital's Young People's Unit. They are planning a short introductory course in horticulture for hospital patients.

Redhall Walled Garden is a beautiful eighteenth century walled garden in Edinburgh within a six acre estate where the Scottish Association of Mental Health offers training in horticulture, conservation, maintenance skills, ITC/admin and life skills for people with mental health problems. This training enables people, over time, to recover their equilibrium. One trainee reports: 'Redhall isn't a life placement, it's a place where you can stop and rest and gather yourself again, learn some skills, appreciate nature, learn that you are still part of the human race and best of all gain ways of coping and nurturing yourself.'[25] Trainees are involved in maintaining the garden, but some also aspire to cultivating their own patch in their own way. This means that there are some raised beds available for individuals to look after.

Learning

Good education should develop people's capacity for thinking, feeling and making – what the famous Scottish thinker Patrick Geddes called 'heart, hand and head'.[26] Allotment sites are good at encouraging a holistic approach which develops various human capacities. Sowing and harvesting, nurturing the crops and the soil all involve planning, observation and decision-making. Working in the rain and sun, listening to the birds and physical labour are sensory experiences. Hand skills are learnt through sowing, planting, working the soil, building compost bins, trellises, huts, brick stoves – all useful and satisfying.

Indeed various professional groups are now aware of how useful involvement in allotments can be for specific client groups or school pupils. For example, Dick Youngson of Nairn writes:

> In our allotment area we have allocated one plot to the health and happiness group for adults with learning difficulties. . . A second area has been allocated to Nairn Academy for their Rural Skills Module students. They have designed their section, grown on bedding plants, developed horticultural skills and planted up vegetables and flowering plants. A third group Junior World playgroup take part in sowing seeds, planting, weeding and harvesting crops. A fourth group, Rosebank Primary School, have set up an eco-school garden in the school property and through our Allotment Society receive lectures and practical help with their science course.[27]

Including children in growing their own produce has become a priority for many local authority education departments. For example in 2004, Balornock Allotment Association and Balornock Primary School decided to work in partnership to develop an allotment as a classroom resource. They involved children in the development of the site, which currently comprises two plots that allow them to grow organic fruit, vegetables, plants and flowers, as well as undertaking other activities such as recycling and environmental projects. Publicity for the project says that the project aims to: 'promote healthy eating and active lifestyles; promote community involvement and responsible citizenship; involve the school in projects that will give purpose to learning and increase pupil motivation.'[28] One of the great features of this type of project is that it fulfils a number of curriculum areas – science, environmental studies and citizenship – as well as linking in with national priorities on health promotion, health education and healthy eating.

On the ground, intergenerational groups such as Playbusters, which enable young people to learn from the skills of the older generation, should become the norm. To be successful they need the input of exceptional people but these can be found in every community. Once a site is established the young people learn the skills required from watching what the experienced plotholders do. Children can also learn these skills from working the plot with their families or in community education plots. Older people can play their role by handing on skills by mentoring the next generation of plotholders, and the local association networks. This is happening across the country and the increased connections and networks are creating growth in understanding and action.

New sites often have demonstration areas so that the allotment site can be used for training and education. For example, Kirkcaldy Community Gardens and Allotments within the Ravenscraig Walled Garden have a training area with raised beds, polytunnels and plots that provides growing space for local schools and community groups.

A place to learn and play

The focus on education and training reminds us that it isn't just adults who benefit from allotments. Children do as well. As was clear from the preceding page, many schools are involved in their local allotment site. However, the main benefits are likely to be outwith a structured curriculum.

In his book *Last Child in the Woods* (2005), the celebrated naturalist Richard Louv argues that today many children spend most time indoors and that this is contributing to the epidemics of obesity, isolation and childhood depression which many of them fall prey to.[29] Even when they do play outside many children spend their time in play-parks on artificial structures or run on tarmac paths in parks. As a result they are missing out on playing in the natural world – collecting bugs, making dens, climbing trees, and disappearing from the adult world. Allotments can remedy that. Some allotment sites have wildlife areas which succour all natural species including children. For example, New Victoria Gardens in Glasgow has a willow tunnel, wildlife areas with shrubs and bushes, space for the children to run and play on the grass and in the trees. It is a site where children can play safely but still find freedom and an outlet for their creativity.

Meeting global challenges

As well as educational spaces, allotment sites are working spaces that contribute to carbon reduction, climate adaptation and food security. They can also play an important part in changing attitudes.

In 2009, an association of village residents in Fairlie in Ayrshire formed the Organic Growers of Fairlie who are all committed to living healthier, more sustainable lifestyles and improving the environment. Ron Gilchrist was a driving force and together with the Growers turned a derelict, polluted, brownfield site into a lovely, peaceful grow-your-own mini allotment garden using innovative composting and vermiculture techniques. Ron Gilchrist had formed a company called Greenway, which has been at the forefront of sustainable food production projects for over fifteen years, developing systems to recycle organic waste, promote soil regeneration and produce wonderful, organic produce – delicious and nutritious – within a socially enriching environment. The Fairlie Growers report tells us:

> Our second poly tunnel (84ft long!) was filled with
> 3 rows of raised-beds and an overhead watering
> system has been installed. Vast amounts of all kinds
> of vegetables have been grown – tomatoes,
> squashes, cucumbers, strawberries, beetroot,
> turnip, basil, runner beans, maize, pumpkins,
> peppers, courgettes, chillies, garlic and aubergines
> are just a partial list. You almost needed a guide to
> find your way through the tunnel.[30]

Carbon reduction, food security and adapting to a changing climate are all priorities for the Scottish Government's Climate Challenge Fund, and are important strands in meeting the challenge of global change. Allotments are eligible for funding in all its categories. Growing and eating your own vegetables and fruit cuts down on imported produce and processed foods. However, plotholders need to vary what they are doing to meet local circumstances. For example, in Ullapool's Riverside Gardens Allotments plotholders preserve heritage seeds to grow Sutherland kale which is adapted to their particular climate.

Gardening certainly makes people aware of the effects of climate change. Gardeners know that earth is much better at draining rainwater than tarmac car parks. Allotments are also an increasingly important resource for wildlife. Many of the plants and animals that struggle to survive on intensively managed farmland find a refuge on allotment sites.[31]

Allotment plots are never monocultural and the diversity of planting across a site ensures there is always food and shelter for the wild inhabitants. For example, the early flowers on gooseberries, the brassica that are left to flower, and the companion plants provide early nectar for the bees. There is also a succession of flowers throughout spring and summer to the brambles and marjoram in October. Stalk and leaf mould are left as havens for insects. Plotholders often have small ponds for frogs and toads. If the site has 'natural boundaries' with trees and hedges these provide green corridors, nesting areas and shelter which are an important resource in the world of tarmac and concrete.

On the carbon reduction front, there have been several studies on the greenhouse gas emissions from growing, marketing, and processing food. It is estimated that some nineteen per cent of total UK emissions are generated by the food sector and that an average person is responsible for 12 tonnes of CO_2 emissions each year and 2.3 tonnes of this will come from food. While 0.4 tonnes is used in domestic processing of food, 1.9 tonnes is due to agriculture, transport, processing, packaging and retailing of our food. Home grown produce avoids these latter emissions because gardeners eat their own vegetables and fruit, usually walk to their plots, use manual methods of soil cultivation and, at best, nurture their soil through a virtuous compost cycle. Experienced plotholders grow green vegetables, herbs and flowers all year round. They harvest and store sufficient potatoes and root vegetables for the year, have soft fruit from May until October and on some sites have apples and pears for the autumn that keep into the winter. If we use conservative estimates we find that at least 1 tonne of CO_2 is saved by each standard allotment plot every year and a one hectare allotment site saves about 50 tonnes of CO_2 per annum.[32]

Experts are beginning to realise the role growing spaces and food can have in mitigating the issues of climate change, resource depletion as well as hunger, obesity, urbanisation and the loss of land. Food was not one of the criteria for the award when Bristol won the competition to become Green City of Europe. The criteria were almost solely based on carbon reduction, however the city's strong sustainable food programme, with allotments as part of this, contributed to its successful bid. Glasgow and Edinburgh are also working towards becoming Sustainable Food Cities but land for growing is central to achieving this as we shall see in a later chapter.

In 2014 the *Journal of Applied Ecology* published a study on allotments which clearly sets out the contribution that they can make to the environment:

Maintenance and protection of the quality of our soil resource is essential for sustainable food production and for regulating and supporting ecosystem services upon which we depend. Our study establishes, for the first time, that small-scale urban food production can occur without the penalty of soil degradation seen in conventional agriculture, and maintains the high soil quality seen in urban green spaces. Given the involvement of over 800 million people in urban agriculture globally, and its important contribution to food security, our findings suggest that to better protect soil functions, local, national and international urban planning and policy making should promote more urban own-growing in preference to further intensification of conventional agriculture to meet increasing food demand.[33]

In 2007 Scottish Natural Heritage (SNH) commissioned a report on 'Growing Nature – the role of horticulture in supporting biodiversity' and they are now involved with health boards in establishing therapeutic gardens.[34]

It is in the interests of all people to care for the earth, the creatures, and plants. Nowadays people talk about this as 'stewardship'. For plotholders this involves an exchange whereby they learn from their plots as well as nourish the earth and their plants.

Spirituality

Traditionally Scotland was a very religious country but not a particularly spiritual one. Nowadays people in various countries are becoming more aware of the spiritual vacuum in their lives which has been created by our exceedingly materialist and ego-driven culture. Spirituality is often defined as a strong sense of connection to something bigger, and more meaningful, than yourself. This is why gazing at the stars, listening to a choir or even being part of a large audience can induce spiritual feelings. Being in touch with nature and the cycle of life can also foster a sense of spirituality. So it isn't difficult to see why for some people having an allotment is nothing less than a spiritual experience. And yet again this is good for well-being. Indeed Professor Martin Seligman, the leader of the Positive Psychology movement, maintains that one of the most important factors for well-being is meaning and serving a goal larger than yourself.[35]

Putting it altogether

So as we have seen throughout this chapter the benefits of allotments are many and varied – mental health, well-being, spirituality, community development, creativity, learning, food production, carbon reduction . . .

A 2012 research paper from Newcastle University looked at the 'social, health and wellbeing benefits of allotments' via their empirical study of five allotment societies in Newcastle. Throughout the report they stress that people particularly benefit from allotments as a result of their increased involvement with community, food and environment. They conclude:

> For many allotmenteers, the spiritual benefits of
> allotment ownership derive from the feeling that
> the site is a haven, an escape from the concerns of
> day to day life. It is, however, a long term project
> that demands commitment and coping with

disappointment as well as success, yet gives great rewards in return. . . Allotment societies build throughout years a social fabric that crosscuts and overlaps with offsite socio-economic status of gardeners. Benefits of allotments go far beyond the boundary limits of allotment societies.[36]

We couldn't agree more.

CHAPTER TWO
This land is our land

Glimpsed from trains in the countryside, hidden behind walls, between tenement blocks and in odd corners of the city, allotments are green oases, still spaces dormant in winter, teeming with life in the summer. As we saw in the last chapter, allotments are more than just a place to grow vegetables: they have always contributed to the social, economic and environmental agenda and to the well-being of the plotholders and local community. Indeed they are already making many communities more resilient and healthy than they would otherwise be. Allotments' capacity to play an important social role was demonstrated in the twentieth century during the two World Wars and the Great Depression.

Allotments – definitions and roots

There are various models for communal growing spaces but the Community Empowerment Bill, currently making its way through the Scottish Parliament, defines an allotment site as an area of land that is subdivided into allotment plots and which may or may not include communal areas and buildings. The dimensions of a traditional allotment plot were measured in rods, poles or perches. These are different names for the same unit and hark back to medieval times when ploughing was done with oxen, chained together in pairs or foursomes. The ploughman handled the plough, and the lad controlled the beasts with a stick which was the rod, pole or perch (5½ yds or about 5 m). The size of a plot was not defined in law but was usually between 200 and 300sq yds (or 10 rods). Today it is mainly accepted that an allotment plot is a piece of land on an allotment site of a standard size of 250m². Fractions of a plot may be made available by agreement at a local level between the local authority (for Council plots) and the plotholders' association. So plotholders may cultivate a full plot, half plot or even a quarter plot.

Allotment land can be owned by the local authority, belong to private landowners, be owned by the plotholders themselves (usually through a trust) or leased from private landowners. The allotment plot is used mainly for the cultivation of vegetables, fruit, herbs and flowers for non-commercial use and leased to individuals, families, groups of individuals and organisations. Because allotment plotholders care for their own patch of land, they have a strong attachment to it. Many sites have been operating for over 100 years and have a sense of history and continuity.

Allotments were originally established to enable families to grow their own food to supplement their diets and provide an outdoor activity for working men which would divert them from pubs. Unsurprisingly, allotment provision significantly expanded during and between the two World Wars and up to the 1950s. The Allotments (Scotland) Act of 1892 'obliged local authorities to provide allotments for the "labouring population"' if there was demand. Then in World

War I, in order to maintain the food supply, the Board of Agriculture obtained powers under Regulation 2L of the Defence of the Realm Regulations, 'to enter on land for the purpose of cultivating it or using it for the keeping and breeding of livestock, poultry or bees, or arranging for its cultivation.' The Cultivation of Lands Order delegated these powers to the country's urban local authorities. Thus during the war as much land as possible was converted to allotments to grow food to supplement shortages. The Defence of the Realm Act also enabled local authorities to commandeer land for wartime allotments.

In the Depression there was even more pressure for allotments. The Scottish Allotment Scheme for the Unemployed was founded in 1931/2 by a Joint Committee of the Scottish National Union of Allotment Holders and the Society of Friends in Scotland, and supported by the United Kingdom government. It was to 'enable unemployed or seriously impoverished men and women to obtain and cultivate Gardens or Allotments Gardens by the provision of seeds, fertiliser at low cost, the provision of tools, help for fencing and equipment of ground for cultivation as Allotment Gardens.'

Again in 1939 war provided the driving force for new sites. The experience of World War I had shown that allotments could play a significant role in the supply of vegetables and soft fruit and help with the supply of meat by the local raising of pigs, hens and rabbits. The Cultivation of Lands (Allotments) (Scotland) Order of 1939, along with Defence Regulation 62A, encouraged local authorities to set up new allotments, leasing land as necessary and giving them the authority to take over unoccupied land.

Additional demand for allotments in Dundee came from different circumstances. In the heyday of the jute mills, women were more employable than men. Their smaller hands and greater dexterity made them well-suited to this work. Meanwhile, unemployed Dundonian men passed their days at the ever-increasing number of allotments which sprang up there. The creature-comfort in some of their sheds bears testimony to the long hours they spent on their plots. Competition among the plotholders abounded and contributed to the rise of Dundee's Flower Show and other shows in the area. Show classes were not only for fruit and vegetables but also for flowers such as daffodils, chrysanthemums and dahlias. Growing for showing is still important for Dundee's plotholders.

Fast forward to 2008 when environmental concerns encouraged the Scottish Government to set up the Climate Challenge Fund to support communities across Scotland to take action on climate change and move to low carbon living. Concerns about food security and the provision of local food were behind the Government's Food and Drink Policy 'Recipe for Success' (2012). This promised to ensure that allotments and 'grow your own' projects are strategically supported, and to produce practical advice and best practice guidance that will appeal to public bodies, communities and individuals to help them develop local 'grow your own' initiatives.

One example of an allotment which has not only survived, but thrived, through periods with differing rationales for plots is Budhill & Springboig allotments in Glasgow. The site has been there since the 1920s so it has existed through hard times, the 'nearly forgotten times' and into the green organic times of today and now has a growing waiting list of keen plotters. So it has sustained itself for nearly a century by building a community of like-minded people, and cherishing the soil and local resources.

The legal position

Allotments have a long legal history though few people realise that there is still legislation covering them. The first Allotments (Scotland) Act was passed in 1892. As we saw above, the legislation was the result of horrendous poverty and the need for ordinary people to have a plot of land to grow food. The Act placed responsibility on the local authority to provide and manage this and on the tenants to look after the land. It provided the framework for Councils to set up allotments. Many Councils never embraced their legal responsibilities under this or subsequent Acts – the Land Settlement (Scotland) Act 1919, and the Allotment (Scotland) Acts of 1922 and 1950. The section of the 1892 Act, still in force in 2014, contains the provision that if six local ratepayers write to the Council requesting an allotment site and 'If the Local Authority is of the opinion that there is a demand for allotments in their area they have a duty, subject to the provisions in the Act, to acquire and let suitable land for allotments.' Despite this legislation in some areas you have to wait seven or eight years for a plot as there is no timescale in the legislation within which the local authority has to meet the request. The Community Empowerment (Scotland) Bill to be presented to Parliament in 2014/2015 will rewrite and update the Allotment (Scotland) Acts and by ensuring that Councils must meet local demand this should mean that allotments will sprout up across the country and that everyone will have an opportunity to garden.

The current provisions which relate to the termination of allotment tenancies apply to private allotments as well as those owned or leased by a local authority. Some sites are owned by plotholders and administered by trusts or by the committee acting as a board and these are completely independent. All allotment sites are, of course, subject to health and safety, and equal opportunities legislation.

Readers who are interested in acquiring a plot should, in the first instance, contact their local authority and ask how they can be put on the waiting list for a site in their area. Depending on the organisation of allotments in the authority (see Chapter Six) they may be put on a central list and/or referred to the local allotment association.

From ancient roots to present flourishing

It is difficult to ascertain when allotments started as they were not really defined until the 1892 Allotments (Scotland) Act. In some areas allotments were first developed as an answer to the problems of post-enclosure rural poverty with employers and landowners providing allotments to 'deserving' labourers.[37] The oldest allotment site in Glasgow that we could find was created as part of a model village for railway employees:

> Cowlairs Works was founded in 1842 at the
> Glasgow end of the new railway from Edinburgh. It
> was the first works in Britain which built
> locomotives, carriages and wagons in one factory.
> In order to attract workers, the Edinburgh &
> Glasgow Railway set out to build a model village in
> Springburn (The Blocks). As well as railway factory
> workers, Springburn provided a home for many
> drivers, firemen, signalmen and guards as well. The

> planned water closets, shops and library never
> materialised, but the allotments, covering about 3.5
> acres, did and remained for more than a hundred
> and thirty years.[38]

In 1947 there were probably about 70,000 plots across Scotland but the 2007 audit 'Finding Scotland's Allotments' identified only 6,300 individual plots on 211 active sites.[39] The Scottish Allotments and Gardens Society believe there are now about 7,900 plots on almost 300 sites. However that is only one plot for every six hundred people in Scotland whereas it is estimated that one in every hundred people would enjoy and benefit from access to a plot. There are long waiting lists in Scottish cities (over seven years in Edinburgh and some parts of Glasgow) and many groups are trying to find land to create new sites.

The number of allotments plummeted in the middle years of the last century. Many sites were lost to building developments but there were other factors. Changing attitudes and lifestyles, more access to leisure activities and a wider choice of affordable produce in the shops also contributed. However, the main reason for the loss of so many allotments was simply because sites had no protection. The Housing (Scotland) Act 1952 trumped any allotment legislation and many sites were sold for housing. Today the Scottish Allotments and Gardens Society are campaigning for 'Allotment sites on local authority or public owned land [to be] deemed permanent and protected from closure. Any on land leased from a private landowner should be subject to a long-term rolling lease and protected from closure.' At the moment most plotholders on Council sites sign a missive each year which is an agreement for one year's tenancy. Plotholders want security of tenure and a permanent site. They have a relationship with the land, rotate their crops, achieve a virtuous cycle of compost and growth and know every corner of their plot. It takes many years to obtain a 'good soil'. Fruit bushes and perennial plants such as rhubarb, asparagus and artichokes need a permanent growing space; they do not give of their best until well-established. However many Council officials and Councillors do not want to lose control of the land; they want allotment sites to be temporary so that they can relocate them if a housing developer appears or they find another use for the site.

An example of a site recently threatened by closure is Kennyhill in Glasgow. It is the oldest in the city and was created in 1917 but in the 1970s the Council planned to close it down to make way for a motorway. Gert Lory led a campaign to save the site and for his successful efforts received a Scottish Allotments and Gardens Society (SAGS) medal for service to the allotments community.

Allotment security is nothing new. Minutes from 1920 for the General Committee of Glasgow Corporation report a resolution from the Glasgow and District Federation of Allotment Holders Associations:

> That this meeting of plotholders and neighbourhoods affirms that the urgent need of the allotments movement is security of tenure and earnestly urges upon Town Councils and Parish Councils the desirability of co-operating with local allotment associations to secure ground on a permanent basis where allotments are on temporary ground only.[40]

The Corporation rebuffed the resolution.

Governments and local authorities continue to like the idea of temporary, rather than permanent sites. In 2014 the consultation on the Community Empowerment Bill contained the suggestion that 'land belonging to a local authority not immediately required for the purpose for which it was acquired can, if suitable, be used for the temporary provision of allotments.'

SAGS recognises the need for plots and the opportunity afforded by temporary sites but has recently reaffirmed its belief that allotment sites should be permanent and that temporary sites should be designated as 'communal growing spaces'. This may not seem significant but it means that the provision of temporary sites would not count towards meeting the demand for allotments in any area.

Stalled spaces, mini-plots and community growing

Allotments also differ from community gardens in that an allotment site contains mainly individual plots. However, a plot may be taken by a community group, usually with a leader working with volunteers. It can also be shared by individuals or family groups. In allotments the responsibility for each plot rests with the individual plot-holder/s and the resultant produce is for them to use or give away as they think fit. In communal gardens the responsibility for all the land and infrastructure usually rests with the members of the management committee or board. The produce is shared. As well as staff members, there are often visitors and volunteers. Volunteers can be from various groups or they can be trainees, service users or people with additional support needs referred by external agencies.

Sarah Robinson is Climate Challenge Officer for a housing association in Glasgow called nghomes. She told us:

> There are clear benefits to housing associations taking on a plot to open up growing opportunities to the wider community. It acts as a training route to support learning for new growers and helps increase confidence in their ability if they want to take it further. This also helps the allotment committee ensure than new plotholders will go on to be productive and have successful plots where in the past many plotholders have struggled on their own and perhaps have been resistant to give up a plot or ask for help. There is also a wealth of knowledge and experience at allotments and I can't speak positively enough about the support and help that Peterhill allotment committee have given to the community plot. This means that the communities on the site are really resilient and able to support each other. In future it would be great to see more dis-used plots utilised by the community projects and hopefully the increased demand for allotments will encourage more land being made available to communities to grow their own, eat more locally, seasonally, economically – sustainably.[41]

A new development in recent years has been the conversion of small spaces into community food growing areas. These are often called allotments when they are actually community growing spaces and the produce is shared among the volunteers who tend them. These small spaces are very useful as they enable community organisations to introduce people to growing and transform derelict land in the area. Shettleston Community Growing Project is an example of what can be done given a dedicated development officer. It opened in 2011 on a quarter hectare site with 50 raised beds, a communal fruit bed, seven hot houses, a wildflower meadow, and a communal area for workshops. It has lots of open days. It now has links to the local school and is embedded in the local community. However, such small spaces do not offer the opportunity for individuals to cultivate a larger plot of ground nor derive some of the individual benefits we identified in the previous chapter.

Glasgow City Council started the scheme 'stalled spaces' in 2010 and now has over 12 hectares leased at a peppercorn rent. However many of these sites are included in plans for future development, although it must be said that it can be over ten years until the development begins. Nonetheless such sites are temporary and, as several community groups have found to their cost, they can be removed at a moment's notice. In Glasgow one small site, after existing for three years, was bulldozed suddenly without any warning. After three years of cultivation another was given a month's notice. 'Temporary' and 'stalled' means temporary.

Edinburgh is piloting 'mini-plots', pockets of unused green land around the capital's housing estates. Again they are not allotments but provide small, usually raised beds for those who wish to grow something but do not have the time or inclination to cultivate an allotment plot. It is led by City of Edinburgh Council managers in the Neighbourhood Communities and the Council itself who wish to save money on maintenance costs and grass-cutting.

Community gardens and 'stalled spaces' are important strands in the vision for a new kind of society which bring people together to celebrate growing and food. They enable people to gain practical horticultural skills and clear up derelict sites. However, by their nature they are transitory, and usually depend on external funding to sustain them. They are a positive development as they can focus energy and enthusiasm, and can create an exciting dynamic involving play, happenings and other community events. On the other hand, they should not be seen as the same as allotments as the latter are permanent and sustainable – at least when permitted by the authorities.

People are now establishing links between community gardens and permanent allotment sites and this allows an exchange of information and resources and enables people engaged in a community garden project to find their own plot if this is what they would like. One of the problems we identify in Chapter Six is that in some urban areas people have not formed associations to seek land and create allotment sites as they have done in smaller settlements and areas. It takes time for groups to form and their dynamics to settle down allowing them to become a functioning, working organisation. Community gardens which bring local people together could provide a nucleus for people allowing them in the longer term to gain the skills and bond which would enable them to form a viable allotment association that could then seek land and funding for development.

How sites have changed over the years

The usual image of allotments is of working men gaining respite in the open air or an opportunity to feed their families. There is some veracity in this image as the standard plot can produce enough vegetables over the year for a family of four. What's more, as we saw above, many allotments came about as a diversionary activity for unemployed men. For example, the Scottish Allotment Scheme for the Unemployed was designed 'so that the physical, mental and moral stimulus of productive work would help keep the unemployed fit for whenever the happy call to resume regular employment may come to them.'

During World War II allotments were a haven for those involved as is seen in Jean McKay's story. Jean was just three years old when her father, a docker, became a plotholder at the South Western site in Glasgow in 1936. Her mother was the real gardener of the family and Jean remembers that in the 1930s, the family spent days on end at the allotment with dinners of tatties, turnip and cabbage cooked on the wood-burning stove: this saved having to use a precious penny for the gas-meter at home. Money was scarce: it was a time of widespread unemployment and great poverty as there was little or no work for the Govan dockers, who spent many of their days playing 'pitch and toss'. During the war, Jean's most vivid memory is being wakened by the warning wail of the air-raid sirens and being bundled into her coat. Instead of going to the nearest air-raid shelter, Jean and her mother carrying her baby, walked from their home in Eaglesham Street up Gower Street and then through Ringwood to their allotment where they lit the stove and settled for the night.

In the past most people thought of allotments as essentially for men but as Jean's story testifies women were often the more keen gardeners in the family. Nowadays there are lots of women involved in allotments both as gardeners and leaders. Indeed the demography on most sites is changing with people from all sections of the community taking part.

Gone are the days when it was only poor folk who worked an allotment – a development which is very good for social cohesion. In an address to the Springburn Area Committee in 2011 Linda Pike explained:

> An allotment isn't just a place to grow spuds. In each and every plot in this country you will find a wide range of people with a breadth of knowledge and experience in many areas, from the unemployed, the disabled, doctors, lawyers, engineers, environmental enthusiasts and kids who want to grow the biggest beanstalk in the world. There are few places where such a diverse mix of the population regularly get together and share information, advice and a cup of tea on an equal footing with each other because at the end of the day everyone is equal in wellies and an old torn jumper.[42]

Another recent development is that there are many people, like Linda, who are aware of the various benefits of allotments. Many of those advocating them nowadays will talk about health, well-being and community as well as the environmental benefits.

Costing the earth?

The cost of a new site depends on the level of services and infrastructure of plots and the sites themselves. A larger site will be cheaper for the services required than a small site. If the Council puts in paths and huts then the cost increases. However under current legislation Councils are only required to give access. Fencing is a very big cost if it needs to be rabbit, deer proof or even 'small-boy proof' but a simple fence with hedging is acceptable unless there is a problem with rabbits or deer. Then there may be the cost of main paths, water and drainage. SAGS assumes an average cost of £750 per plot but this can be reduced to zero if plotholders are just leased the land. It can cost £2,500 per plot for a well-serviced site.

Mark Thirgood obtained a £101,370 grant from the Climate Challenge Fund for a site at Killandean, West Lothian in 2013. He reports that 'For a 25 – 50 plot site, development costs are likely to be in the region of £2,500 – £3,000 per plot (2013 figures). This may sound a lot, but remember you need to allow for sheds, community facilities, communal tools and other bits and pieces; as well as fences and paths and car parking.'[43]

To increase provision and enable one in a hundred people in Scotland to have a plot requires in the region of 44,500 new plots. If we assume a mixture of standard plots (250 sq m) and half plots then this would require about 600 hectares. This is about the size of eight and a half golf courses. Ideally everyone should have access to a plot within walking distance of their home but in some regeneration areas the potential land may be contaminated. The Cabinet Secretary Nicola Sturgeon reported at the SURF conference in May 2013 that as part of the latest funding 200 hectares of land had been remediated and we suggest that such land could be used for allotments. Glasgow needs about 50 hectares to fulfil the aim of one plot per hundred people so even if all these were provided on contaminated land, the area required is still only a quarter of what has been reclaimed already.

A 2010 survey found that out of the 32 Scottish local authorities ten either had no Council allotment sites or did not manage any that there were.[44] However, this is now changing and authorities are looking for land and taking a growing interest. Glasgow has created five new sites in the last three years and Edinburgh has a policy of one new site each year. In their response to changes in allotment legislation, Aberdeenshire Council recommended:

> For new housing developments LAs should require
> an allocation of sufficient land for allotments/
> community food growing. Sites should be situated
> in close proximity to other amenity open spaces to
> allow for flexibility of use. Aberdeenshire's Open
> Space Strategy states 1 plot (200m^2) per 50 people.
> For existing developments and settlements a
> retrofit is likely to provide a significant challenge.[45]

There's no doubt that the current tide is in favour of those wanting to see more allotments in Scotland and that this is something of a challenge for all local authorities as Sandy Paterson, Allotments Officer for Glasgow City Council points out:

> There has been an increasing awareness of
> environmental issues in the last 10 years or so and
> as people realise the beneficial impact allotments
> can have on mind, body and budgets the demand
> for a plot has never been higher. Whilst this is
> welcomed by this local authority it brings with it
> significant challenges, namely availability of suitable
> land, competing priorities on diminishing budgets
> and increased costs associated with allotment
> provision.[46]

CHAPTER THREE
Digging, dreaming and surviving

Plotholders all share a passion for the land, the plants and the other inhabitants – the birds, bees, and foxes. Every site is different, every plot unique reflecting the skills and interest of the plotholders. Full of untold stories, they are an unrecognised community resource. Interest is growing but how can we ensure an adequate supply?

Finding suitable land is the biggest challenge to satisfying the need for allotments. Although there appears to be an abundance of potential sites, the stark reality is that very few of them are ultimately available or suitable for the purpose. In many cases, aspiring plotholders come up against obstacles such as land banks, local structure planning zones, or contaminated soil.

In the past allotments have often been offered on marginal land but this is more difficult with urban development. Some professionals argue that any new developments should have allotments as part of the brief. We agree with the Scottish chartered surveyor, Steven Tolson, when he suggested that:

> Given that development land is ultimately finite, suburbs will need to be built to higher densities and be more urban in character. Having greater

densities will require appropriate space. Policies should not be merely to seek a percentage of ground for open space but a more considered view of how such space should be used. This means rather than space being dedicated to play, rest and modest ornament we should also consider how some of this space can be used for cultivation. Cultivation should not be seen purely for growing things but also how we use this activity for the benefit of exercise and social interaction.[47]

Nonetheless, despite the difficulties, there are examples of new flourishing allotment sites where, with determination and goodwill, suitable land has been found. The support of local authorities in making land available is essential in urban areas. Edinburgh City Council is leading the way on this. It recently surveyed all its land holdings and identified 25 potential sites.

Here are a few more recent, and encouraging, examples:

- Tollcross Park in the east end of Glasgow had 418 plots in 1918 but over the next decade, these were slowly closed for other activities or developments such as a bandstand. However in 2011 Glasgow Parks department resuscitated part of the original site and they now have 42 plots of different sizes. This is still a long way from the original numbers but is a good start.
- In 2007 Comrie Development Trust acquired 90 acres from the old military camp at Cultybraggan with the aim of developing the site as a model of sustainable development for rural communities across Scotland. Allotments were set up in 2008 as part of the Cultybraggan Food Quadrant and 30 plots have now become a flourishing part of the development.

- In 2010 the Shettleston Housing Association responded to a demand from local people who were keen to see a community allotment in the Shettleston area. The housing association made land available for the site and provided staff support to develop the project, alongside community partners and Glasgow City Council. They also secured funding from the Climate Challenge Fund to establish 50 raised beds. These were necessary as the site is on derelict ground.

However, while there are lots of great new projects we also need to be vigilant and organised to ensure that existing allotment sites are not lost to building development. Some allotment holders formed the Nairn Allotment Society in 2005 after they realised that their plots were included in an area of land to be developed on the western edge of Nairn. After a vigorous campaign, the Nairnshire area committee of Highland Council agreed in principle to enter into a management agreement with the Allotment Society. The Society had to wait until March 2007 before the agreement became a reality but from that time the organisation moved forward with a five year management plan, obtained funding from a variety of sources and now has two satellite allotment sites in the area.

Social justice

Access to land to cultivate, care for, and grow food is a social justice issue. The neighbourhood statistics for Glasgow in 2007, where people often live in tenements or high rise flats, showed that in some places only six per cent of the population had access to a garden and that 84 per cent were without a car. In 2009 the Scottish Allotments and Gardens Society (SAGS) and Scottish Natural Heritage (SNH) analysed the access to allotments in Scotland against the Scottish Index of Multiple Deprivation.[48] (See Table 1 below.) This confirmed that with fewer plots accessible per person there is less opportunity to garden in deprived areas. Since other statistics show that up to 70 per cent of the population enjoy gardening this is clearly a social justice issue. It also means the priority must be to provide allotments in some of the most deprived areas of the country.

Table 1: Access to gardens in Glasgow

Area	Population	% Children	Flats	Without car	No. in houses with gardens	Access to gardening
Glasgow	609,370	20.4%	73%	67%	162,000	27%
Bridgeton	7,113	19.2%	88%	84.2%	435	6%

Sorting out planning

Many people are in principle happy to welcome the establishment of new allotment sites but, in reality, when they are asked if they would support a new site on a specific piece of ground close to their own home, they change their opinion. Residents may fear that an allotment site will become an eyesore which could adversely affect their neighbourhood. Other objectors cite such things as noise, increase in traffic, and bonfire smoke.

In 2012 in Strathblane, Blanefield in Stirlingshire there was an acrimonious battle in the community over a proposal to open allotments on the Duntreath Estate. There were 42 individual objections as well as a petition listing 290 signatures. However, there were also 106 letters in favour and a 294 signature petition. Objectors were worried that the site would look –

> . . . untidy and cause disruption to a quiet area through noise, smells, bonfires, rubbish and music. The objectors also claimed wildlife could be disturbed and that there could be safety issues for children, cyclists and walkers due to increased vehicles using a former disused railway line track to access the site.[49]

Strathblane Community Council supported the application, provided measures were put in place to address access, traffic and management issues. As a result of the antagonism the landlord withdrew the field he had been offering for an allotment site but later came up with another. The Council granted planning permission and the allotment site was duly created.

In general, groups which have successfully converted potential objectors into supporters have worked hard to ensure that all their local community is involved in the plans. This can simply mean listening to concerns and taking appropriate measures, or, as in some sites in Fife, welcoming local residents onto the site by giving them a key. In fact as we shall see more fully below locked allotment gates are not always required.

If the look of the site is the main problem then objectors could be asked to look at the independently managed Dean Gallery allotments in Edinburgh. These were once the kitchen garden to an orphanage and have no huts at all as everyone shares an old brick-built shed embellished with Ian Hamilton Finlay's artwork. At Town Yetholm in the Scottish Borders, the site includes the remains of the oldest building in the village which has been sympathetically re-roofed and brought back to life as a potting shed for plotholders. New sites in Glasgow and Edinburgh often have small sheds, providing storage for the plotholders' tools and accoutrements, but as we are about to see this uniformity comes with a big price tag.

Huts

Building huts, particularly using recycled material, is a creative and meaningful activity. That plotholders can do this in walking distance from their dwellings, and recycle local resources, provides a deep and satisfying activity. A good Scottish hut with an easy chair, stove and frying pan, the heat from the stove warming the grapes in the adjacent greenhouse, is something many aspire to. In the Old Craigie Road allotments in Dundee there are enormous wood-piles that fuel the huts all winter. Many plotholders there have solid fuel stoves and calor gas bottle conversions which warm them and their glass houses. On a chilly spring morning we met four men happily sitting round their stove eating bacon butties.

Landscape architects and Council officers are often wary of such anarchic constructions but they give undeniable pleasure to those lucky enough to inhabit them. Sadly, the opportunity to have a proper hut is being lost in many new sites where the Council is providing standard, pre-fabricated huts and glasshouses which do not allow any diversity. The officers justify the sanitisation of sites because of the modern perception that the landscape should be neat, uniform and controlled. While we agree that some hut building can be excessive and there is a tendency for some plotholders to hoard 'good recyclable stuff' there should be a middle way that allows the basic nest-building instincts to be realised. If local people are affected by the view of the sites there can be a compromise and agreement on location of huts or even no huts. To satisfy everyone's needs there should also be sites, perhaps screened or hidden, where more innovative construction can take place.

Access and open gates

Rural sites in Ullapool, Town Yetholm and Lochaline have open access so that anyone can walk round the site any time they want. Hamiltonhill in Glasgow opens every Saturday in the summer, encourages potential plotholders to help with the site maintenance and has many links to other organisations and local schools. However, apart from formal open days, plotholders in Scotland are often wary of strangers visiting their sites and lack the trust found in for instance the Nordic Kolenhaven, outlined in a later chapter, where sites are open daily in the summer months. Access is a dilemma for allotments because while sites need to be seen as inclusive and open and not seen to be hiding behind locked gates and barbed wire, there is often a history of vandalism and plotholders fear losing their precious produce.

The issue is also pertinent for new sites. For example, the access officer at Stirling Council was relaxed about a locked gate to stop fly tipping and addressed the security worries which arose from a few incidents of vandalism. However, the association is in the process of negotiating a lease and the Legal Services department of the Council has overruled the access officer and its staff are insisting that the gate should be left unlocked. Here's what a Policy Manager in the Scottish Government advises:

> In my view the local authority is obliged to provide access to allotments to tenants by suitable paths and roads but is not obliged to grant unrestricted public access to the site. However, the local authority could seek to make it a term of any lease relating to the site that there was to be such public access. It would be up to potential tenants whether or not to enter a lease on those terms.[50]

We believe that as allotments have more community plots and as every small community obtains its own site, allotment associations will allow their gates to be open during the day.

Reaching the sites

Provision of vehicular access and car parking for an allotment site depends on its geographical location, public transport links, and how far away the plotholders live. Planners and local residents unfamiliar with allotments sometimes assume that the number of cars accessing the site will be far greater than it actually is. Plotholders do not all want to visit their plots at the same time of day and most sites rarely have more than two or three cars in their car park even at weekends. Many plotholders can walk to their plots and for some there is no parking close to their sites anyway. Access to the Perth Working Men's Gardens on Moncrieffe Island in the Tay is via a metal footbridge adjacent to the railway line so they have no vehicular access and neither do the plotholders on the Dunblane allotments who walk along the river banks.

However, where possible, access for the occasional seasonal bulk delivery of compost or manure is appreciated even if it is not possible for a lorry to access the site itself. In any case plotholders are adept at informal organisation: at Musselburgh, for example, a human chain can relay 500 bags of mushroom compost on to the site in the minimum amount of time and helpers find it an enjoyable, communal activity.

Turnover

The turnover of new plotholders is often high. There are a number of reasons but foremost is the realisation that time and hard work are needed to produce results. Small starter plots are being introduced on some sites for those reaching the top of a waiting list so they can gain some experience and be sure that taking on a whole plot meets their expectations.

Many of the old established sites have plotholders who have been gardening there for decades, but finally give up because the physical effort becomes just a bit too much. When they give up their plots, their experience and guidance, not to mention their company, is lost. As well as starter plots for newcomers, small plots and seats are welcome additions to many sites where older plotholders can 'downsize' but continue their long association with their site to everyone's advantage, particularly in passing on some of their skills to newcomers.

Jenny Mollison, one of the authors, feels very strongly about the need to cater for people's changing circumstances so we're giving her a soapbox:

> For every person who gives up an allotment plot there's a queue of others waiting to take their place. However, behind each vacant plot lies a story. Some plotholders will have been forced to hand in their key having fallen short of the required standards of cultivation. Others give up because of changed domestic or job circumstances and some people move away. But there is a special group of people whom I would love to retain on the site. These are the time-served plotholders. Many of the old established sites have plotholders who have been gardening there for decades, who finally give up because the physical effort becomes just a bit too much. It can be a wrench for them. My former neighbour Willie continued to grow 10 metre rows of swedes long after there were enough people in his family to do them justice. He was generous enough to hand some on to other plotholders, but the rest just ran to seed and ended up on his compost heap. Eventually, the effort to keep up his own high standards became too much and he gave up his plot. I feel that if he'd been offered the opportunity to downsize he would have jumped at it. He would have welcomed the transition from hard physical labour to something gentler while retaining the benefits. On sunny days he could have made his way up to the site, got his hands dirty in the soil, had a blether and a seat in the sun. For our part, when Willie and others in similar circumstances give up their plots we lose their experience and guidance, not to mention their company. I would love to see some small plots and well-placed seats becoming the norm, alongside the

starter plots for newcomers, where our older
plotholders can continue their long association
with their allotment site to everyone's advantage.

Creating raised beds can be one way to help people stay
on. For example, Inverleith in Edinburgh have just built
twelve raised beds and Stuart Mackenzie reports that:

One lady is an ex-plotholder that had to give up her
plot due to serious ill health. She asked the
Allotments Officer to reallocate her old plot but
keep her on the list in case she was ever fit enough
to come back. She's now got two carers looking
after her and all three are so happy to be able to get
gardening again on our raised beds. It really is
fantastic to help people like her that would have to
just pack it all in if they couldn't dig anymore.[51]

Bringing people together

Events such as Potato Days with a variety of seed potatoes for
sale, workshops and seed swaps bring plotholders together
in shared interests. These can be one-off events or more
regular. For example, some associations participate in local
horticultural clubs that pool resources and experience,
disseminate information and technical knowledge among
their members and exchange seeds, produce, tools, and
ideas. The Scottish Allotments Conference in June each year
combines a good mix of horticulture and politics. Politicians
and eminent gardeners both have their space as do
plotholders reporting on successes and problems from
round the country. These are simple events which cost little,
but bring together those with a shared interest to meet and
talk and grow the community.

The growth in community plots and the engagement with plotholders has opened up channels to the wider community. For the past nine years Joyce Gibson has worked as a part time gardening tutor with the Glasgow Simon Community (GSC) – an organisation working with people who are homeless or have been affected by homelessness at some stage in their lives. Many are recovering addicts and have suffered mental or physical health problems and appear to have low self-esteem. Joyce has taught them how to grow fruit, vegetables and flowers on an allotment in the Oatlands area of Glasgow. Recently she has been working on another project for the Simon Community which has involved visiting the accommodation projects within GSC and identifying ways in which the outside space could be utilised more by residents. Working closely with one of the support workers and residents from a project in the east end of Glasgow, Joyce created an allotment in a back garden. At another project in the south of the city raised beds were built and food crops grown in an area of back garden. Once again the staff and service users were involved. Joyce, a plotholder herself, is thrilled at these types of developments as she can see how allotments can benefit the wider community.

Allotments provide a space in which old and young can come together whether children accompanying their grandparents to sow seeds and pick peas on the plot or in a wider context for bringing together members of the local community. For example, Playbusters, mentioned in Chapter One, runs inter-generational projects in the east end of Glasgow and have a plot in Westthorn allotments. Andy Forrester is the local community activist and is an inspiration to people in the area. He spends many hours coordinating the project and working with adult volunteers and young people of all abilities. He shows them how to take care of the allotment which teaches them patience and encourages them to adopt a healthy lifestyle. Local people can also access a growing space which helps them learn about environmental issues, growing vegetables and healthy eating.

Community Service Orders, as an alternative to custody, offer some offenders the opportunity to engage in gardening work. This work involves discipline, regular attendance, and satisfactory work performance and is generally carried out by small groups under the supervision of a Task Supervisor. Some allotment associations which have become involved find that the offenders quickly acquire skills to perform useful tasks which would not otherwise have easily been carried out by plotholder volunteers. In Musselburgh, where the Task Supervisor is a highly regarded member of the local park staff, the arrangement works to everyone's advantage with the offenders' contribution to the tasks in hand being welcome. In other areas, the same confidence and trust in this system has not yet been established and there can be anxieties about the likelihood of increased vandalism and theft from the site by the offenders involved in this payback scheme. However, as people see how service orders have worked well in other areas they may become less reluctant to involve offenders in their sites.

Finally, allotments can also help with the integration of asylum seekers as they can bring together people from all walks of life and provide a platform for the sharing and dissemination of knowledge at a local level. However, more needs to be done to recognise this potential, and encourage and assimilate asylum seekers and immigrants into allotment sites.

Avoiding conflict in the allotments

Allotments are a microcosm of the world. There are power struggles, harassment and intimidation on some sites but when acknowledged these can provide an opportunity for people to learn the skills of conflict avoidance and resolution, negotiation and participation. These are skills which are being lost in our increasingly fragmented and polarised world. Allotment association members also need help with governance and capacity building but, having acquired them, they can share these skills in other areas of life.

So what are the issues that are most likely to cause conflict?

• **Criticism of plot cultivation:** How a plotholder cultivates their plot is an expression of their individuality, often the only chance they get to indulge in the creative process. Plots range from the traditional plot with four equal areas for crop rotation to a cottage garden type of mixed beds. However, some plotholders can have very strong views on how an allotment plot should look, what should be grown and how it should be cultivated. When this is communicated, criticism of your plot can seem like an attack on yourself!

• **Warnings and eviction threats:** Sites often have a site committee that sends out warning letters and eviction notices if a plot is not being cultivated. Sometimes inaction is because a plotholder has given up and not told anyone. However if they appear intermittently and 'do a bit' then the way can be to open for conflict. Associations are supposed to have site rules but the phrase 'a plot should be weed-free and fully cultivated' is open to interpretation. Problems also arise because the site committee may not appreciate the stress that individual plotholders are under. There is often a feeling that every plotholder must be treated the same unless they have explicitly explained they have physical or mental health problems. For many their plot is an escape from stress but they may not have much time to cultivate it. Bad weather or family issues may disrupt gardening plans and the weeds do not wait. When the plot inspection letter arrives it can be the last straw causing resignation or rage. It is reckoned that 80 per cent of vandalism on allotment sites, such as burning huts, has been carried out by fellow plotholders as a result of friction on a site.

• **Huts:** As we saw earlier in this chapter, huts are an opportunity for creativity but they are undeniably a big source of conflict with many people in the area saying they make sites look like 'shanty towns'. Most Council or allotment association rules have a limit on size and shape of sheds, but the problem is how to enforce such rules in a small organisation: people are reluctant to remove their treasured construction that has taken many hours to design, often from recycled parts, and many more hours to build. Resentment grows.

• **Committee coup:** It is unusual to find a committee that has not experienced a coup or a removal of office bearers. It is only recently that good governance for allotment associations has been encouraged and advice available from the Scottish Council for Voluntary Organisations, SAGS or other local groups. Old constitutions enabled the committee members to remain in position for long periods. This is fine if the plotholders are happy with the way things are run and most just want to cultivate their plots and not worry about the running of the site. However, new people may want to change the ethos, perhaps to encourage tighter plot inspections and enforce the rules. Or they may want to engage more with the local community or even question the use of site funds. Threats and criticism, hurt feeling and being unappreciated after years of effort, combined with loss of status, cause resentment. Site events such as work parties or open days also cause problems if some people don't participate.

Sharing a plot: The plot is supposed to be cultivated by the named plotholders and not passed on to friends or relatives because this means they are 'jumping the queue' but people can be struck down with physical infirmity and need help. What's more, families may want to participate and friends may want to share the experience. Some Councils do not permit joint tenancies because of perceived problems with responsibility for the upkeep of a plot. However, many sites allow friends or partners to have joint missives as long as this does not enable anyone to bypass the waiting lists. Joint missives mean that if a plotholder dies or gives up the plot for any reason then the other person who has tended the plot with them can continue. On one site where the plotholders bought the land, people assumed the plot was theirs and sold it on in a local pub. If more asset transfers of land for allotments takes place in the future, the plotholders involved with such organisations must understand the restrictions and responsibilities imposed by community ownership.

To sum up, allotment associations and allotment forums are becoming aware of the conflict that can arise and are now encouraging ways to avoid and address it. With increased use of the Internet there is a greater opportunity for communications among plotholders and transparency about what is required, what is being done for the site and how plotholders can meet and work together. All of this may help mitigate conflict.

Set up and running costs

In the previous chapter we looked at the cost of setting up an allotment but there are also running costs. Private established sites have shown over many years that they can maintain themselves and flourish. They sell produce and home baking at open days, hold raffles and use the in-house skills of their plotholders to maintain the site. However, on local authority sites there is often a landlord-tenant relationship with an expectation that the Council will maintain the infrastructure and provide water, skips and support.

For the individual plotholder there is an initial cost of tools and then an ongoing cost of seeds, manure, netting etc. as well as rent. Some of this outlay will be recovered from the savings on produce. Allotments will not provide all the food a family needs although Peter Wright, who weighed all his produce over a number of years, has shown that a good gardener can provide most of the vegetables for a family of four throughout the year. Altering his planting pattern could provide more fruit and maybe fewer vegetables to complement or enhance the diet throughout the seasons.

Shopping at major supermarkets to purchase the best bargains may provide cheaper fruit and vegetables if the total cost of the allotment is counted in. However the 'two for the price of one' and similar offers contribute to the vast quantities of food which goes to waste. Food waste is an anathema to most plotholders who plan their meals round what's ready for harvesting and take home exactly the quantity required. As Linda Pike, the vice chair of the Glasgow Allotments Forum, says:

> Allotment holders very quickly get into the idea of eating seasonally. I rarely buy any vegetables now as my family take advantage of what we have at the time and manage to provide a year round supply of veg and fruit and when there is an abundance that even the neighbours can't consume then you freeze, pickle, preserve, dry or store.[52]

Diversity

'Every site is different' was the comment again and again after the visits to twelve sites in Glasgow organised by the Glasgow Allotments Forum and Glasgow City Council over the summer of 2013.[53] That is the challenge and charm of allotments, they enable ordinary people to express their individuality and work together in an informal, unstructured way that generates creativity. Sites develop and change with the people and the seasons. New blood with new ideas can upset the established dynasties as we saw earlier, but change also brings people together. Because allotments are a source of 'slow growing' they can, in good circumstances enable all the plotholders to appreciate and accept difference whether of race, gender or disability and can lead to lasting friendships.

CHAPTER FOUR
Harmony with the soil

The Earth Charter 'is a declaration of fundamental ethical principles for building a just, sustainable and peaceful global society in the 21st century.' The Charter sets out clearly that the Earth is 'our home' and that:

> The resilience of the community of life and the well-being of humanity depend upon preserving a healthy biosphere with all its ecological systems, a rich variety of plants and animals, fertile soils, pure waters, and clean air. The global environment with its finite resources is a common concern of all peoples.[54]

Many of those involved in the allotments movement are seeking to raise awareness among plotholders of environmental challenges as well as highlighting how much plotholders already contribute to a more sustainable and resilient way of life.

Working with the elements

John Reid dedicated his work *The Scots Gard'ner*, first published in 1683, 'To all the Ingenious Planters in Scotland'. More than four hundred years on and Scottish allotment gardeners continue to come up with the most ingenious solutions to a whole range of elemental difficulties.

Good soil is one of the fundamental necessities for growing fruit and vegetables. However, not all our new sites have been blessed with this. In Chapter One we saw how the Organic Growers of Fairlie acquired a derelict, polluted, brownfield site and so had to garden mainly in raised beds with a growing medium resulting from innovative composting and vermiculture. Raised beds are also a necessity on both the Comrie and Ullapool sites where the soil is very shallow.

Water is another necessity to successful gardening but even where there is a close supply of mains water, connection costs are prohibitive. Yetholm Yewtree Allotments rely on water harvesting from all available pitched roofs on their site and at Dunblane water can be pumped from the river which runs past the site. As well as lack of water, excess can be a problem. Raised beds can get round the problem of an area prone to occasional flooding.

In her Merlin Trust report Caitlin DeSilvey described the allotments at Paterson Park in Renfrew and the ingenious solutions to their problems:

> Paterson Park is in the Clyde River floodplain.
> Every spring during the March neap tide the water
> rises well above wellington boot level. One year, an
> old allotmenteer who had been sleeping in his shed
> woke to find his cat floating away on a cushion.
> When the floodwaters subside, the gardeners hurry
> to prepare the soil and get their seeds in the
> ground so they can harvest a reasonable crop
> before the floods return in September.

Once the dry days of May arrive, gardeners have a few source options for their water needs. Many of the plots are fitted with wells and small pumps that tap into a constant subterranean flow. Others rely on rainwater, collected through elaborate gutter systems into fifty-five gallon barrels. 'If a man can't figure how to get a barrel for free he shouldn't have an allotment', decreed Bert (the Chair of the Association).[55]

The sun provides several allotment sites with a welcome source of power. Enthusiastic and knowledgeable do-it-your-selfers have installed solar panels at two Edinburgh sites, Midmar and Inverleith, with great success.

Strong winds can cause havoc but with a little forward planning in the layout of the site and the early installation of appropriate windbreaks, the effects of wind can be reduced. Hedges seem the obvious solution but they take a while to grow so, in Shetland, old car tyres have been built into protective walls round a site, and planted up so as to minimise any adverse visual impact. They also have a special design for their polytunnels to protect them against wind damage.

Working in harmony

Increasingly plotholders are rekindling the importance of working in harmony with the natural environment. Between 2005 and 2007, groups in Glasgow, Edinburgh and Tayside all published booklets on 'Allotments and Biodiversity'. These highlighted that allotments bring people and nature together, are important habitats for local wildlife and help to maintain and conserve biodiversity both above and below ground. Organic gardeners depend on the natural environment for their produce and in return provide food and habitats for numerous species as well as conserving the soil. Nature conservation groups such as Froglife, Bumblebee Conservation and Butterfly Conservation all work with allotment associations to encourage them to build ponds, plant fruiting shrubs and boundary trees, construct wood-piles and be aware of insects' needs throughout the year.

The SAGS newletter in 2012 carried this message:

> When gardeners think about pollinators they tend
> to think about domestic honey bees. But in fact,
> according to the Bumblebee Conservation Trust,
> our native wild bumblebees pollinate a much wider
> range of the crops grown by allotment gardeners.
> Unfortunately modern horticulture techniques are
> destroying the wild flower habitats which the
> bumblebees love, and bumblebees are in decline.
> Allotment gardeners can help by planting crops
> with nectar rich flowers. For example, bumblebees
> love most of our standard herbs, and there is surely
> room for a little herb garden on most plots.[56]

Keeping bees on an allotment can be a rewarding pastime and helps to enhance local nature. Many allotment crops depend on bees for pollination. The City of Edinburgh Council has drawn up some helpful management rules for keeping bees on allotments.[57] They recommend that aspiring beekeepers should be members of the Scottish Beekeepers Society and pass the Basic Beemasters' Certificate before embarking on keeping bees on their allotment. Some sites will not be suitable for beekeeping due to the proximity of public footpaths or houses. Other sites may be too insecure and would leave hives vulnerable to vandalism.

Decades ago a common allotment practice was keeping

livestock. Wartime plotholders kept rabbits and chickens and bees were commonplace. The practice died out but is now back on the agenda. The current shortage of allotments, as well as the decrease in the size of some plots, means that using allotment space to keep livestock is not usually allowed. Some of those running associations think it is less important to keep chickens, for example, than it was years ago. Free range eggs from one's own hens are delicious but they are more widely available in shops nowadays than they were years ago. What's more, hens are untidy eaters and hen food attracts vermin. Nonetheless an increasing number of plotholders want to keep chickens. This can sometimes cause problems when too many hens are confined in a small space. However, chickens are becoming increasingly popular and Glasgow City Council has pilot projects on a couple of sites and is planning to produce a policy and guidelines in the near future.

On the bandwagon

Plotholders in Glasgow are demonstrating how allotments can contribute to a more sustainable lifestyle. This is happening as a result of Glasgow's Green Sustainable Allotment Award which was created in 2010. The prize is a trophy commissioned from Lotte Glob (an eminent Scottish ceramicist). The award is to celebrate the contribution that allotment sites in Glasgow make to 'the Sustainable City' and to publicise good practice.

The trophy was awarded to four different sites between 2010 and 2013. Each of the winners was judged to have contributed to sustainability in different ways but each demonstrated how they met the criteria by caring for the earth, sustaining the plotholders by looking after and co-operating with each other; and sustaining the wider community through, for example, sharing with local people.

In the 'caring for the earth' criterion, the judges considered whether the site overall was a rich, well-managed space with diverse planting providing food all year round for people as well as having ponds, fruiting hedges and flowers for the bees, butterflies and birds and compost bins, water butts and green manure planting to minimise waste.

In the 'sustaining the plotholders' section judges considered whether the site was a 'community growing space' with different sizes of plots and raised beds; whether it welcomed and supported schools, community groups, people with special needs, individuals, families and friends; had a vibrant association with people participating through group maintenance of the site, social events, parties for plotholders' children; and was an inclusive space with good communication through newsletters, websites and notice boards. In a nutshell they were looking for a site where people talked freely, experienced gardeners shared their skills, and where children were welcome and those in difficulty supported.

Under the 'sustaining the wider community' heading, points were given for visits from local schools and older groups, composting workshops, gardening clubs for non-plotholders, children's parties, open days, gardening events and a 'Friend of the Allotment Site' scheme for neighbours and ex-plotholders. In short, was the allotment site a dynamic hub for the local neighbourhood?

Judges found that no one site contained all of these

features but that many aspects of sustainable growing are found in allotments across the city. Therefore they suggested that rather than giving one award every year to the 'most sustainable site', all the allotments in the city should be asked to assess themselves on the sustainability criteria and then decide whether they are at bronze, silver, gold or green level. In 2013 fifteen sites participated and there were two bronze, eleven silver and two gold awards across the city. The ultimate aim is for all allotment sites in the city to participate and show how allotments really contribute to 'Green Glasgow' and the aims of the Earth Charter.

Site design

Awareness of being part of a bigger picture comes early to aspiring plotholders when they are faced with designing their new site. Most new groups of potential plotholders will have experienced the excitement of obtaining a piece of land for their allotments after months and sometimes years of searching. However, once the euphoria has subsided, they will have to devise a workable plan which makes the best of the site. Visiting established sites should be a prerequisite for all new groups. Gut feelings about the essential components have to be translated into acceptable plans. The practicalities of gardening in harmony with nature include making the most of the sun and minimising the effects of wind. Finding out how others have achieved their dreams or overcome obstacles is often inspiring and educational. No two allotment sites are exactly the same, but many features will be similar.

We are aware that landscape architects who are unfamiliar

with allotments often place undue emphasis on neatness and unnecessary hard landscaping thus driving up the cost and making later adaptations to the site difficult. We recommend Scotland's Allotment Site Design Guide as it is a good practice guide covering the establishment of a new site or the regeneration of an old one.[58]

Tailoring the site to the best advantage for growing crops is just one aspect of the job. Local residents and community groups will also be interested particularly in its appearance and how it integrates into the landscape as well as the inclusion of facilities of which they can take advantage.

Compost, urine and recycling – the virtuous circle

Allotment sites have always been the exponents of recycling with traditional plotholders taking pride in never wasting but recycling. A new skip in the neighbourhood is seen as a potential source of useful materials rather than as a repository of unwanted goods. It can generate almost as much excitement as a newly discovered source of manure.

Compost is essential for good soil and is easily made, as Peter Wright from Edinburgh explains in very jovial terms:

> We all have a responsibility to reduce waste, and making compost is one way. We all probably know how to produce a good compost, with a good mix of green and brown waste. My brown waste is torn up egg boxes and the paper from our document shredder. I get a perverse pleasure from hearing the machine chew its way through bank statements and bills. No sticks or woody plants unless they have been through the shredder (not the document

one!!), no diseased vegetables and plants, (these are best burnt or put into your household brown bin for central composting where the higher temperatures can kill off the disease). No cooked food or waste meat, rats and mice are attracted to your compost and once established they are extremely difficult to get rid of. Even the green cones recommended for food waste are not immune from attack by vermin.

Regular turning and aeration, is very necessary, as is the addition of accelerators, a spade full of earth, limestone, and the magic ingredient, the amber nectar, urine. Male gardeners are uniquely endowed to collect their urine in those large plastic bottles. And I collect several litres per week, which get taken down to my allotment to go onto my big compost heap or into the compost daleks in our small back garden where the household waste is recycled. There I have three plastic compost bins, when the first was full, the dalek was lifted off and the half rotted compost turned into the second, the first bin was then filled with new waste. When it was full, the second dalek was turned into the third, and the first into the second. When the first was full again the third had superb crumbly compost ready to go onto the plot. The urine gets poured onto the compost in the first and second daleks.

Reading a National Trust for Scotland newsletter I was intrigued by their article on 'outdoor peeing'!!! The article went on to say that peeing on the compost activates and accelerates the compost process and saves water. What was not mentioned was the energy saved.

The water used to flush your toilet is treated to drinking water quality, using energy not only to purify, but also to pump it to your house. The wastewater has to be treated at the sewerage works before being put back into rivers or the sea, again saving energy. So save your 'P', pour it on your compost heap or into your daleks, and pride yourself that for each non-flush you have saved one lot of water, two lots of energy, and made the best compost ever.[59]

Recycling in all its forms – whether urine or materials – is all-important on the site. As Linda Pike points out this is second nature to plotholders:

Allotments, community gardens and local growing projects are hives of ingenuity when it comes to recycling. Everything has a second, third and so on life until it rots back into the soil. I have rarely seen a shop bought hut or greenhouse on a plot and I'm glad it is so as not only are our structures much more environmentally friendly they are unique reflections of their owners.

Rainwater collection and composting of plant materials are second nature and many of us work closely with local companies who will deliver old pallets, unwanted used timber, logs, bark, chippings and much more that we will turn into a thing of beauty and usefulness as opposed to a spot in a landfill site.[60]

However there can be a downside to all this activity. As Dundee City Council advises:

Items which you may wish to bring from home to make your allotment shed more homely such as kettles or chairs, will inevitably break or outlive their usefulness. In such cases you should again bear in mind that if you managed to bring it in, you should manage to take it away again and dispose of it responsibly.[61]

Widening horizons

Allotments have always evolved. For example, in pre-war plots in Glasgow's Queen's Park, Irish immigrants only grew potatoes and cabbages until their wives demanded flowers. But there's little doubt that changes in produce have speeded up in recent times. Migrants from abroad often crave their home food and are amazed at what can be grown in Scotland. Plotholders from other countries bring with them a bit of their own culture. This can manifest itself in both their style of gardening and what they choose to grow. This can then provide further inspiration for other plotholders. An Italian, Ricardo Paganucci, arrived in Musselburgh in the early 1950s to work as a building site labourer. Marrying a local girl, he settled in the area but a bit of his heart remained in his homeland. He also longed for its food. A big part of his enjoyment from his allotment came from being able to grow those Italian plants, particularly salad greens, which reminded him of his origins in Italy.

African greens, Indian herbs and Chinese roots can all help newcomers settle. Growing their home produce, however small the quantity, engenders well-being that can offset the effects of Scotland's cold and rain. Everson from Lambshill Stables allotment site in Glasgow was amazed to find the greens from Zambia grow very well in Glasgow and is now hoping to set up a market garden supplying African vegetables. Dave Sheriff has grown plants from round the world on his plot in Garscube, Glasgow, including achocha (cyclanthera species) and cape gooseberry (physalis peruviana) from South America, lab lab beans (dolichos lablab purpureus or hyacinth bean) from South East Asia and even watermelon (citrullus lanatus).

Tariq is an ebullient Dundonian whose parents came from Pakistan in the 1960s. His mother and father were from a rural community and needed their plot to grow their traditional food. As a young lad Tariq was dragged in to help because 'families work together'. Today he enjoys the plot and is now 'dragging' his son in to help. He and his parents grow Asian vegetables and herbs particularly fenugreek, coriander, radishes, garlic onions with spinach, rape seed, potatoes and chillies. These are for the traditional dish Saag but they also cook with new vegetables such as turnips. When we visited in April, Mooli was flowering. It isn't just the roots which are used but also the seed heads which are used in pakora and chapati. On Sundays he often meets with other plotholders to banter and share food such as his chicken curry. Tariq says he really appreciates the plot, finding it a stress release from working in his three shops which are in three different towns. He says that it brings a new perspective on the world, awareness that nature is part of being a human being. It also gives him an awareness of God and that 'it pushes a human being down from where they think they are to the realisation they are as insignificant as an ant.'

Voodoo horticulture

One of the differences between gardening in the seclusion of one's own garden and gardening on an allotment is that there is usually a ready supply of established gardeners keen to advise on everything from planting times and methods to seed varieties. Sometimes the advice seems contradictory ranging from the traditional double-diggers to the new-fangled no-dig system with a smattering of permaculture and bioplanting by phases of the moon added in. There are recipes for making liquid composts from all manner of plant material such as nettles and comfrey. As the new plotholder's confidence grows, and some of these methods are tried out, it becomes apparent that they all have their merits and it's a question of adapting them to suit. Tolerance is one of the features of allotment gardening even if some of the practices appear to have more to do with the occult than science.

Eco gardening

Increasingly some plotholders are aware of permaculture and the permaculture principles:

> Permaculture is a creative design process that is based on ethics and design principles. It guides us to mimic the patterns and relationships we can find in nature and can be applied to all aspects of human habitation, from agriculture to ecological building, from appropriate technology to education and even economics.[62]

The ethics of permaculture – earth care, people care and fair share – form the foundation underpinning the Glasgow's Green Sustainable Allotment Awards. The seven domains of permaculture action (Nature stewardship; built environment; tools and technology; culture and education; health and spiritual well-being; finances and economics; land tenure and community) are driving new visions for growing and development of allotments not just across Glasgow but Scotland and the world.

In 1972 the Declaration of the United Nations Conference on the Human Environment stated:

A point has been reached in history when we must shape our actions throughout the world with a more prudent care for their environmental consequences. Through ignorance or indifference we can do massive and irreversible harm to the earthly environment on which our life and well being depend. Conversely, through fuller knowledge and wiser action, we can achieve for ourselves and our posterity a better life in an environment more in keeping with human needs and hopes. There are broad vistas for the enhancement of environmental quality and the creation of a good life. What is needed is an enthusiastic but calm state of mind and intense but orderly work. For the purpose of attaining freedom in the world of nature, man must use knowledge to build, in collaboration with nature, a better environment. To defend and improve the human environment for present and future generations has become an imperative goal for mankind - a goal to be pursued together with, and in harmony with, the established and fundamental goals of peace and of worldwide economic and social development.

To achieve this environmental goal will demand the acceptance of responsibility by citizens and communities and by enterprises and institutions at every level, all sharing equitably in common efforts. Individuals in all walks of life as well as organizations in many fields, by their values and the sum of their actions, will shape the world environment of the future.[63]

Plotholders are contributing to these aims by caring for the earth, acquiring skills in growing in harmony with nature and – perhaps – cultivating an enthusiastic but calm state of mind!

The best allotment associations realise that they can play a significant role in rising to the challenges posed. We can maintain and improve the capacity of our small patches of earth to produce vital, renewable resources for future generations.

CHAPTER FIVE

Connections

The international movement of allotments has origins across the world. The concept of land set aside for the general population, in particular the labouring poor, may have started in Ancient Rome, but in the centuries that followed there was no uniform approach to the allocation of land or the design of allotments. Different approaches depended on the history, culture, heritage, religious traditions, economic resources, climate, geographic condition and the political patterns of the people. In the United Kingdom the Enclosure Act of 1806 prompted the authorities in the village of Great Somerford in Wiltshire to set land aside for allotments with five to six acres out of the 970 acres enclosed.[64] This was the first time this had been done.

The following examples show how allotments are integrated into the landscape in different countries and the impacts allotments have on the lives of the people.

Nordic examples

Scandinavian allotments began for the same reasons as the UK but have followed different models. The Danish Garden

Allotments Association has 420 allotment garden associations with 42,000 members so this provides about one plot for 133 citizens.

The allotment gardens near Hjelm near Aabenraa in South Jutland were established in 1821. They are considered to be among the oldest in the world. Historically, as in other countries, parcels of suburban land were leased out so that factory workers could escape cramped unhealthy living conditions. Today there are two different types of allotment sites in Denmark: one is like the traditional Scottish model with plots of land primarily for growing food and the other follows the Norwegian Kolonihager model.

An example of the latter is Århus's Skovlunden's beautiful allotment garden which is situated in verdant surroundings behind Marselisborg Castle, near the city centre. Information on the site tells us:

> The association has 133 gardens with small houses which can only be bought by people who live in flats and have no garden. Each garden is around 400 m², although some are a good deal larger. Owners are allowed to live in their simple houses throughout the summer when the association's main water tap is on. There is no water in the area during the winter and it has no sewage system, the lavatories being emptied by a gully emptier. Some owners have installed their own solar arrays on the roof, while the rest of the association's members do without electricity. In times past, the gardens constituted a necessary larder, where people grew their own vegetables for consumption back home in flats. These days, it is the simple life in the allotment garden association which attracts people. There is, for instance, no prospect of electricity

being installed in Skovlunden. Life in the allotment garden association is all about unwinding, getting away from stressful urban life and enjoying the countryside. In Skovlunden they do so among more than 1100 apple trees, 850 gooseberry bushes and some 1150 raspberry bushes. The allotment gardens have become status symbols, according to the association's chairman Frank Karlsen. There are 1200 people on the waiting list for an allotment garden, of whom 300 are actively looking. On average, six allotment gardens are sold every year.[65]

In Oslo in 1907, 130 plots were laid out on the city's old landfill site at Rodeløkka. Every political party in the City Council elections that year applauded its creation and supported the establishment of more Kolonihager in their manifestos. The membership list shows the majority of the garden's pioneers belonged to the skilled section of Oslo's rapidly growing working class.[66]

In Stavanger, a recent survey of housing shows 61 percent of existing residents live in block housing and flats, so in this part of Norway at least, the Kolonihager are still needed by those without gardens.

An American example

America may be the land of hyper-consumerism and fast food but the current First Lady, Michelle Obama, is doing her best to foster healthy eating. Her book *American Grown* (2012) is about the recent growth of community gardening in the United States and speaks about the community spirit which accompanies developing communal growing spaces for fresh produce.

In Boston the City Fathers have pledged to make Boston a city where every resident has the opportunity to garden in their own neighbourhood. In short, 'community gardens', which are essentially what we would call allotments, are now a core part of city planning. Boston's vision for its community gardens is very similar to the Scottish Government's vision for allotments. But, as we are about to see, the difference is that in Boston vision and advocacy have been translated into action.

There are now almost as many gardens as there are playgrounds and basketball courts. These community gardens are seen as a critical public resource, essential to public health and the quality of life of the Boston resident. The Boston Community Gardens Strategic Plan states:

> The communities with gardens have active citizens
> and strong neighborhoods; the gardens are at the
> center of communal efforts, some political, many
> social and educational. They are one of the largest
> volunteer constituencies in Boston, and a large
> percentage of these people vote. It is not surprising
> that Boston's elected officials support community
> gardeners and actively seek their endorsement. In
> 2008 these officials all proudly wore the title of
> 'Openly Green.'[67]

This commitment means that allotments are built into the greater development plan for the city. With support from the city for infrastructure, community gardens are self-managing and built on the principle of public stewardship. All of the gardens have a strong organisational structure, with both good leadership and the involvement of the gardeners. These garden groups are supported by organisations and informal networks which provide resources when needed. It is this co-operation that is so important for the smooth functioning of allotments and enable them to reach their full potential.

Allotments play a key role in making Boston a vibrant multi-cultural city that brings together people from all walks of life. They are also used by groups throughout the city to bring people together. For example, according to the Asian Community Development Corporation, the Berkeley Street Community Garden is:

> . . . the most visible and vibrant ongoing expression of authentic Asian culture anywhere in the City of Boston. Much more than any "gateway" or restaurant could be, this garden and the Asian gardeners are a living expression of an agricultural heritage that originated over 50 centuries ago in China and continues today here in our city. The elderly Asians intensively farm many of the garden plots and for them spending time in these garden plots is a vital element of their emotional and physical well being and the food they grow contributes to their and their families' nutritional security.
>
> The Asian gardeners create lush and abundant hanging gardens with vegetables growing under, along and over beautiful trellises. The Asian gardeners are predominantly elder Chinese whose daily lives are sheltered in a sphere of Cantonese or Toisanese. In the isolating environment of an English-speaking society and an American culture, the Gardens are profoundly important for the mental and physical health of these elderly gardeners from the Chinatown community. Their garden plots are a beautiful voice to communicate with neighbors different from them in so many ways but in the Gardens so much alike.[68]

The Cuban experience

In 1991 Cuba was suddenly plunged into its worse economic crisis since the 1959 revolution as a result of the collapse of the Soviet Bloc and its economic support as well as the tightening of the USA's economic embargo. Cuban agriculture, which was highly mechanised and dependent on chemical inputs from the Soviet Union, suddenly had to deal with a reduction of over 50 per cent in oil, fertilizer, and pesticide imports. Food imports also reduced. Indeed Cuba's total import bill shrank by up to 70 per cent between 1989 and 1993. As Fidel Castro himself stated in 1991: 'The food question has become the number one priority.'

The food shortage inevitably led to lots of food growing initiatives. People themselves started to use their balconies and back gardens to grow food. In Havana itself urban agriculture took off. This ranged from private gardens to state-owned research gardens. Havana's popular gardens ('huertos populares') became widespread. These are small parcels of state-owned land cultivated by individuals or community groups. They still exist but were first introduced in response to the ongoing food shortages. These popular gardens range in size from a few square metres to three hectares. People can obtain land for gardens through the local government body at no cost, as long as they use it for cultivation. The gardens are usually organised around a household, but it is not uncommon to find arrangements in which more than one household share a garden. This can mean from one to seventy people working the site. They cultivate a wide selection of produce depending on family needs, market availability, suitability of the soil and locality. In addition to vegetable and fruit cultivation, some popular gardens also cultivate spices and plants for medicinal purposes. Today more than 50 per cent of fresh produce consumed in Havana is produced within the city itself. [69]

These popular gardens achieve high yields with minimal external inputs as they apply the principles of organic agriculture. Inter-cropping is commonly practised, and sometimes vegetation stories used with taller trees and plants acting as a protective canopy for lower crops.

The popular gardens have not been problem-free. Some major constraints included the scarcity of available land in densely populated areas; the scarcity of water, particularly during the dry season from November to April; the poor quality of urban topsoil, which is often littered with garbage, glass, and shards of concrete and other building materials; plant disease and pests; and the theft of garden produce, which was rife during the period of ongoing food shortages.

In the early days the gardeners had several resources to help address their problems. They often organised themselves into horticulture clubs to provide support but also to organise regular watch duties to guard gardens from robbers. MINAGRI also provided advice and disseminated knowledge based on the principles of organic agriculture. They also played a pivotal role in the start-up and functioning of the popular gardens and horticulture clubs. MINAGRI also set up centres to sell agricultural supplies to the public that would otherwise be difficult to obtain during the 'Special Period,' such as vegetable and medicinal seeds and seedlings, biological pesticides, organic fertilizer, and tools.

Reports on the success of Cuba's agricultural policy show that the popular gardens revitalized many traditional crops, (particularly starchy root crops) and helped to reduce dependency on outside food sources. In addition to increased food security, the gardens also empowered many individuals and communities. They renewed solidarity and purpose among Cuban communities and this helped to sustain morale during the economic crisis.

England and Wales

There are a number of similarities and points of difference between allotments north and south of the border. For a start the movement in England started far earlier than it did in Scotland and there has also been much more research into allotment history and what is currently going on. Most notable here is the publication of David Crouch and Colin Ward's book *The Allotment: Landscape and Culture* (1997).[70]

In England and Wales the Allotment Acts are broadly similar to those for Scotland apart from the fact that Councils are permitted under the Allotments Act of 1922 to spend 0.8 per cent of their rates on allotments. Legislation also makes a distinction between statutory and temporary sites. The disposal of allotment sites has become the subject of a new Guidance Note from the Department of Communities and Local Government. It tells us:

> Councils cannot dispose of statutory allotment land
> without the Secretary of State's consent. Section 8
> of the Allotments Act 1925 states – 'Where a local
> authority has purchased or appropriated land for
> use as allotments the local authority shall not sell,
> appropriate, use or dispose of the land for any
> purpose other than use for allotments without the
> consent of the Secretary of State'.[71]

Nonetheless despite these differences in legislation, the English and Welsh allotments followed a similar pattern to those in Scotland with peaks of activity in the First and Second World Wars and revivals of interest in the 1970s and 1990s.

In 1998 the House of Commons Environment, Transport and Rural Affairs Committee produced a seminal report entitled 'The Future of Allotments'. It found the lowest level of allotment provision since before the 1887 Allotments Act with only 250,000 plotholders. However, even that low number provides one plot for every 50 households whereas Scotland currently has one for every 600 households. That's a huge difference. Many people's ambition in Scotland is one for every one hundred households so even if we obtained this it would only be half the English rate. Indeed there are more plots in Newcastle or Birmingham than in the whole of Scotland.

In leafy Cambridge there is one plot for every 70 people on 22 allotment sites, eight of which are managed by the Council and 14 which are independent and run by allotment societies. Even so in 2008 there was a petition for more plots and in 2012 the Council agreed to fund 67 new plots and allocated £15,000 (or £224 per plot). Birmingham has 7,584 plots on 115 sites (1 plot for every 140 people) but in 2013 had 1000 vacant plots despite having a long waiting list for some sites. The biggest site has the most vacancies and this seems to be because people favour smaller sites which are more easily managed and where there is greater community feeling and commitment.

In their book on allotments Crouch and Ward highlight the problems with security of land outside the Council sector.

The landowners include British Rail, British Coal, and British Waterways and many of their sites have been transferred or sold to local Councils. The Charity Commissioners remain responsible for many thousands of allotments in England and Wales and while they are required to act within the guidelines of the original trusts that endowed the land for allotments, they can 'make changes particularly where the original trust is for the benefit of the poor . . . such benefit can be conferred in some other way than the provision of allotments'.[72] This provision makes many allotment sites very vulnerable.

England and Wales share common problems to those encountered in Scotland as the organisation and design of the sites is similar both sides of the border and does not reflect continental experience. Fluctuation in demand in England as here seems to come from an initial enthusiasm from the perceived benefits of gardening which is then undermined by the vagaries of the weather and new plot-holders' lack of skills.

The National Society for Allotments and Leisure Gardeners estimates that although there are now approximately 330,000 allotment plots in the UK, to meet the current demand we need at least another 90,000.

International movement

There are a variety of international allotment organisations. The most important European one is the Office International du Coin de Terre et des Jardins Familiaux. It was founded in Luxembourg in 1926. The national federations across Europe which participate in this international organisation has more than 3,000,000 affiliated members in fifteen countries.

The organisation supports the Earth Charter and is very conscious of its international environmental duties.

CHAPTER SIX
Organisation and influence

Allotment associations can face the same challenges as any collective, particularly in finding people willing to take responsibility and contribute to the wider community. People are also busier than they used to be with many more calls on their leisure time. It is often assumed that people know each other and can form a group which will then acquire land, get funding and create a site. This can happen fairly easily in rural areas and small settlements. However, in an urban environment people often have never met and do not know each other. This may explain why, in spite of large waiting lists in urban areas, the acquisition and creation of a site is usually left to the Council or driven by a sympathetic Community Council.

Associations may also have difficulty finding a viable committee. The skills needed to form associations are quite demanding. Finding a treasurer often proves difficult, although the duties are less arduous than sometimes imagined. The essential task involves keeping an up-to-date record of the site's finances as well as an audit trail for all transactions.

Many sites now no longer have a traditional committee structure with only a few office bearers. They now break down the tasks so that as many people as possible are involved. For example, instead of one secretary there may be a membership secretary responsible for the waiting list and informing new members; a correspondence secretary dealing with outside inquiries and, if it is a local authority site, being the point of contact for the allotments officer; a minute secretary; a maintenance officer looking after the infrastructure and organising work parties to keep the boundaries and communal areas in good order; a newsletter editor to keep the rest of the plotholders and wider allotment community informed about what is happening on site; and an events organiser, responsible for open days and other visits. Nowadays it can be useful to have a website 'geek' who can facilitate good communication inside and outside the site. There will also be representatives appointed to participate in the local federation or forum. Spreading responsibility for all these tasks as well as the traditional treasurer, chair and plot inspection team ensure as many people as possible are involved in the smooth running of the association and helps to prevent cliques forming and conflict arising.

Local authority organisation and strategy

Local authority sites are all run differently depending on the history and culture of the different authorities. Edinburgh, Glasgow and Fife have dedicated allotment officers. In the Highlands allotments are part of the Policy Officer for Health Improvement's remit while in Dundee the responsibility lies with an officer in the environment section of the Council.

In the last few years many Councils have approved allotment strategies often under the heading of green space.

95

Edinburgh published its first allotment strategy in 2002 and is now implementing the second one. Glasgow's Allotment Strategy for 2009–2013 has been successful in raising awareness of allotments, creating five new sites and improving several established sites. However the Allotment Mentoring Group which oversees action for the Strategy has not been so successful. It has just been reformed to try to bring together representatives from the different Council departments such as planning, community education, and 'the Sustainable City' initiative together with representatives from housing associations and the NHS. However, given the pressure on Council services and the lack of resources, staff may find it difficult to always dedicate the time required.

Management issues

At the moment local authority sites may be run through direct, devolved or a hybrid management system. Other sites which are leased or owned are independently managed.

In Edinburgh the local authority sites are all directly managed whereas Glasgow and Dundee have a mixture of direct and devolved management. Under direct management everything, including maintenance, is managed centrally by the local authority. This helps to maintain allotments as a priority within a local authority and may assist in securing capital and revenue budgets for investment and repairs. However, the local authority has to collect every individual rent and is responsible for pursuing non-payment of rent. Site inspections can either be the responsibility of the Allotment Officer or the associations.

Devolved management of allotments describes the situation where some measure of responsibility for collecting rents and maintenance rests with the local association. This tends to encourage plotholders to be more self-sufficient and increases their sense of ownership. Devolved management associations may also have better access and be more creative when seeking external funds for improvements.

In Dundee each association has an individual lease, normally of ten years, which is negotiated through the Council's City Development Department. In most of the allotment leases there is a responsibility on the City Council for the maintenance of fences and internal paths and this is important in reducing the costs which have to be borne by the site association.

Sites that lease land through their associations or own the land outright are completely responsible for the management and upkeep of the site. Around a quarter of all the sites in Scotland are independently owned which shows how sustainable and resilient many of our allotments are.

Development Trusts such as those in Comrie and Wellhouse and housing associations with small sites can take overall responsibility for their organisation. Exciting and fertile channels for cooperation are opening up between allotments and separate community growing projects, housing associations and the NHS. In 2006 Reidvale Housing Association signed a 20 year lease with Glasgow Council for the creation of allotments on land near the housing project. They obtained funding and constructed the site which is now run by an independent allotment users group, the Reidvale Community Allotments.

How partnerships work

Local forums and federations which bring together sites and plotholders for mutual benefit are fundamental to the growth of a sustainable society but these can face problems with membership and collective decision making. Edinburgh, Glasgow and Fife each have a good allotment strategy which underscores the need for community involvement and participation. However, all tackle this is in different ways. In Edinburgh, all Council plotholders are members of FEDAGA (Federation of Edinburgh and District Allotments and Gardens Associations). The structure for the organisation is shown below.

Figure 1: Structure for Federation Edinburgh and District Allotment Gardens Association (FEDAGA):

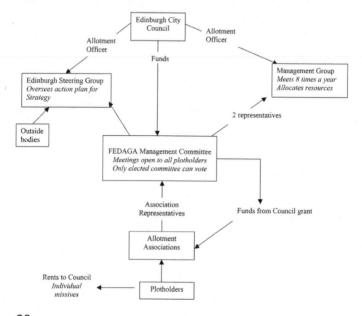

Glasgow manages things very differently. GAF (the Glasgow Allotments Forum) provides the opportunity for plotholders from the different sites across the city to meet, share information and discuss issues related to allotments in Glasgow.

Figure 1: Structure for Glasgow Allotments Forum (GAF):

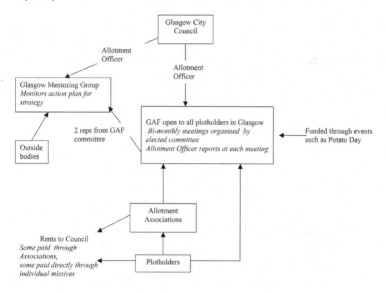

Both the approaches of FEDAGA and GAF have strengths and weaknesses. For example, FEDAGA representatives have a direct input into the budget and dissemination of funds but no devolved management of sites. All Glasgow plotholders have direct access to the Allotments Officer through the Forum but no budgetary input.

Local authority and future structures

The traditional landlord/tenant relationship cannot be sustained in the current economic climate. In future allotment associations will be expected to take more responsibility for themselves. However, this raises problems of changing attitudes, (the usual tanker analogy comes to mind), capacity building for the office bearers and costs. There are a number of private sites across Scotland that have managed and funded themselves for many years and can provide models of good practice. A group in Glasgow is currently exploring the benefits and problems associated with the mutual status which was the organising model in the 1930s. This has the advantage that the association is incorporated so does not face the liability problems associated with unincorporated associations (which is the norm for most Council and private sites). This is also an advantage for Community Interest Companies (CICs) and Scottish Charity Incorporated Organisations. The cooperative ethos echoes the underlying ethos that exists in most sites anyway and a grouping around a local area would enable nearby groups to share training, management and resource support. Fife is exploring the CIC route with three hubs (Glenrothes, Dunfermline and Kirkcaldy) and satellite associations benefiting from closer involvement.

How people can influence decision makers

The current Community Empowerment Bill should provide the legislation for local communities to work with their Council in providing new sites where there is a demonstrated need. But this is only part of the story. It is apparent that confusion often arises when campaigning groups and individuals have little or no understanding of the way in which national and local government functions. Grappling with the distinctions between the role, power and functions of different levels of government for the first time can be bewildering.

The ordinary man and woman in the street should be encouraged to engage with the planners. We need partnerships between local authorities and local people working together, appreciating that our land is precious and can easily be damaged and contaminated by development. We also need them to develop a vision for the sustainability and quality of their neighbourhoods.

In a submission to the Glasgow & Clyde Valley Strategic Development Plan Linda Pike of the Glasgow Allotments Forum said:

> The strategy seems to concentrate on big business, large infrastructure and renewables. At no point do we get the feeling that the man and woman on the street are being seen as just as vital a tool in the strategy as well as the major potential beneficiaries. Would it not be prudent to look at how the provision of useful open spaces, community facilities and food growing opportunities would impact on the health, wellbeing, cohesion and prosperity of communities not only now but for generations to come? This would not only be a very cost effective way of delivering high impact social benefits but would make us all feel that we were integrated into the improvements as opposed to being told what was good for us.[73]

We need to create a dynamic, critical mass of information and support for allotments and other growing projects across

Scotland. We're pleased to say that this has already begun via organisations such as Nourish, the Fife Diet and Trellis. Local food networks are springing up. Allotments are on the fringes of this activity. The Scottish Allotments and Gardens Society (SAGS) which represents plotholders in Scotland is run completely by volunteers, as are the federations and individual allotment associations. SAGS campaigns at national level for allotments and runs an annual Scottish allotments conference that brings plotholders together to share information. SAGS does not have 'a spokesperson' or leader: it is simply a group of passionate, committed individuals all contributing their skills and experiences of actually tending their plots and working in their local associations. They have a wealth of information and contacts but, unlike many voluntary organisations, have no paid staff, volunteers nor premises. Similarly the allotment federations in Edinburgh, Glasgow and Dundee work with the allotment officers on developing the strategy in their authority, provide support and discuss local issues. This is all that plotholders usually want. Sites that have active members can raise funds for themselves. The independent sites that have existed for decades are usually very happy to run and maintain themselves and to deal with problems which occur internally.

As Sandy Paterson, Glasgow's Allotment Officer, points out:

> ... to ensure allotments are sustainably managed for the benefit of all, now and for future generations, improvements can and must be made. This can be achieved by partnership working with a broad spectrum of stakeholders to bring the expertise and resources to achieve increased awareness of issues relating to allotments and building the capacity to meet the challenges head on for the benefit of all involved with allotments.

In this way the great tradition of plot holding can be continued from current custodians to a new generation of plot holders eager and ready to accept the challenge and enjoy the fruits (and veg) of their labours.[74]

CHAPTER SEVEN
Leaving an inspiring legacy

In the previous chapters we have told the story of Scottish allotments and their inhabitants – hidden places for laughter, food and solace; all different, full of creativity and self-expression with the potential to change people's lives. There is no blueprint for how we can build on the opportunities that allotment sites and plotholders offer. Any change depends on recognition of the needs, capacity and actions of the individuals in the local communities. Successful outcomes will arise from actions by, and partnerships between, individuals, local allotment associations (established and nascent), federations, the Scottish Allotments and Gardens Society, local authorities and the Scottish Government.

A shared vision

At the moment there are so few allotment sites that plots are places for the lucky few. For the furtherance of social justice, equality, and well-being there should be a drive for more allotment sites that include individual plots, community plots, and children's areas.

Recommendation 1

The Scottish Government should articulate a clear vision for allotments in Scotland, reflecting good practice from around the world, and subsequently embraced by Scottish local authorities and embedded within Scottish culture.

Development plans, land and strategies

If the SAGS' target of one plot for every hundred people within walking distance of their homes is realised within the next ten years this would make a significant contribution to the nation's well-being. For this to be realised land has to be identified and acquired and existing allotments protected. This will need funding, particularly to decontaminate some of the potential land, but this is mainly a matter of will and agreement.

Recommendation 2

Potential land for allotments should be identified as part of all audits of green space and become a central component of all Local Development Plans and protected for this purpose. Allotment sites on local authority or publicly owned land should be permanent and protected from closure. Any on land leased from a private landowner should be subject to a long term rolling lease and also protected.

Growing partnerships

There should be clear pathways, information channels, and mentoring and training schemes so that individuals and groups who want to have their own allotment or participate in their local allotment community have the opportunity, knowledge and skills to do so. Allotment associations should support the marginalised such as those who are physically and mentally disabled, young people, the elderly, asylum seekers and the unemployed.

Recommendation 3

Once the Community Empowerment Bill comes into force, the Scottish Government should work with SAGS, local authority officers (perhaps through the Association of Public Service Excellence), the NHS, education departments and other relevant organisations to develop guidance notes and information on the implementation of the allotments section in the new legislation. Allotments should also be included in the Scottish Government's national indicators 'Scotland Performs' as well as given specific recognition in Single Outcome Agreements and in relevant strategies and action plans.

Local organisation – hubs

Allotments need a new vision and structure, integrating them into the plans and organisation of the local community thereby making the most of their potential for changing the way our society functions and the experiences of ordinary people valued. There is no 'one model' for this. Just as every allotment site is unique so every local structure will be different. However, challenging and debating the current management model may help with this shift.

Recommendation 4

Local authorities, SAGS and the relevant organisations should form forums, or 'hubs', with local allotment associations to find the best management model for their area. These hubs should produce and disseminate information about successful partnerships and future initiatives.

Last words

Finally, we are aware that for allotments to thrive we need a shift in contemporary Scottish culture and attitudes. As there is a great deal of pressure on funding, resources, and land we will only see a lot more allotments if there is widespread acceptance that they are attractive places both in form and function; places that we value. This will require a sea change in the perceptions not only of landscape architects, local authority officers, and politicians but also the general public. And that means all of us.

The good news is, as we've seen throughout this book, the tide is beginning to turn. Support and interest in allotments may not be back at the high water mark of the wartime era but it is steadily rising. Some of this is coming from the contemporary emphasis on well-being and mental health but much of it is environmental and linked to the desire to grow more local food. For everyone's sake we need to preserve the land we have and involve future generations in working in harmony with it.

Finally, we would like to give the last word to the Diggers of the 17th century as their ballad contained the powerful rallying cry: 'With spades and hoes and plowes, stand up now, stand up now.'

Notes

To read these notes with hyperlinks to most of the articles
and reports listed go to the *Raising Spirits* section of
www.postcardsfrom scotland. co.uk

1 The photographer Carlo D'Allessandro visited Scottish
   allotments to document plotholders and their stories in
   2011 for a touring display, created for the Heritage of
   Glasgow's Allotments and is now held by Glasgow
   Allotments Forum and Scottish Allotments and Gardens
   Society.

2 Phil Hanlon and Sandra Carlisle, *AfterNow: What's next
   for a healthy Scotland?* Argyll Publishing, Glendaruel,
   2012.

3 Carol Craig, *The Great Takeover: How materialism, the
   media and markets now dominate our lives*, Argyll
   Publishing, Glendaruel, 2012.

4 Alf and Ewan Young, *The New Road: Charting Scotland's
   inspirational communities*, Argyll Publishing, Glendaruel,
   2012.

5 Mike Small, *Scotland's Local Food Revolution,* Argyll
   Publishing, Glendaruel, 2013.

6 Tony Miller and Gordon Hall, *Letting Go: Breathing new
   life into organisations*, Argyll Publishing, Glendaruel,
   2013.

7 Theodore Roszak, 'The Nature of Sanity' in *Psychology
   Today*, 1 January 1996.

8 Richard Louv, *Last Child in the Woods*: *Saving Our*

Children from Nature-Deficit Disorder (Paperback edition), Algonquin Books, Carolina, 2005.

9   J. A. Russell and A. Mehrabien, 'Some behavioral effects of the physical environment', in S. Wapner *et al*, *Experiencing the Environment*, Plenum, New York, 1976.

10 Frances E. Kuo and William C. Sullivan, 'Aggression and violence in the inner city: Effects of environment via mental fatigue', in *Environment and Behaviour*, Vol. 33 No. 4, July 2001, pp. 543–571.

11 For an overview of this type of research go to the Environment section of the Centre for Confidence and Well-being's website – http://www.centreforconfidence.co.uk/flourishing-lives.php

12 Stephen Kaplan, 'The restorative benefits of nature: Towards an integrative framework', *Journal of Environmental Psychology*, (1995) 15, pp. 169–182.

13 Caitlin O'Brian DeSilvey, 'To all the Ingenious Allotment Gardeners in Scotland', Merlin Trust, September 2001.

14 Richard Mitchel, speech at Faculty of Public Health Conference, November 2013.

15 Jenny Mollison, *The Scotsman*, March 23, 2013.

16 See, for example, Edward Deci and Richard Ryan's Self-Determination Theory. http://www.selfdeterminationtheory.org

17 For information go to: http://www.sags.org.uk/weblog/?p=15

18 For information on fruit and vegetable consumption in Scotland see Scottish Health Survey 2012 main report.

19 See NHS Greater Glasgow and Clyde news release retrieved from: http://www.nhsggc.org.uk/content/default.asp?page=s1192_3&newsid=15544&back=s8_1

20 See North Glasgow Community Food Initiative information retrieved from: http://www.ngcfi.org.uk/id13.html

21 See *The Independent*, 16 February 2014.

22 'Finding Scotland's allotments 2007', Scottish Allotments and Gardens Society.

23 Juliet Josse Johnson, 'How does taking part in a community allotment group affect the perception and social inclusion of participants?', dissertation for BSc (Hons) Sheffield Hallam University, 2006–2007.

24 Go to: http://www.trellisscotland.org.uk

25 Quoted in on-line article retrieved from: http://greenflagaward.org/news/2012/09/redhall-walled-garden-quite-literally-saves-lives/

26 You can find a short overview of Patrick Geddes's work on the National Library of Scotland's website: http://www.nls.uk/learning-zone/politics-and-society/patrick-geddes

27 Quoted in Scottish Allotment and Gardens Society report retrieved from: http://www.sags.org.uk/docs/Reports Presentations/nairn08.pdf

28 Promotional newsletter retrieved from: http://www.scdc.org.uk/media/resources/what-we-do/demonstrating-links/bugs_briefing_note.pdf

29 Richard Louv, *Last Child in the Woods, op. cit.*

30 Report on Organic Growers of Fairlie's website: http://www.organicgrowersfairlie.co.uk

31 See wildlife on allotments at http://www.naturalengland.org.uk

32 Tara Garnett, 'Cooking up a Storm: Food, greenhouse gas emissions and our changing climate', Centre for Environmental Strategy, University of Surrey, September 2008.

33 Jill Edmonson *et al*, 'Urban cultivation in allotments maintains soil qualities adversely affected by conventional agriculture', *Journal of Applied Ecology*, 24 April 2014.

34 SNH Commissioned Report 244: Growing Nature – The Role of Horticulture in Supporting Biodiversity, 2007.

35 M. E. P. Seligman, *Authentic Happiness*, Simon and Schuster, New York, 2002.

36 M. Ferres and T.G. Townsend, Global Urban Research Unit electronic working paper No 47, School of Architecture, Planning and Landscape Newcastle University, p. 45.

37 See Caitlin O'Brian DeSilvey, 'When Plotters Meet: Edinburgh's Allotment Movement 1921–2000', University of Edinburgh, 2001, M.Sc.

38 See http://gah.org.uk/GeneralGlasgow/ThePast.aspx Heritage of Glasgow's Allotments www.gah.org.uk

39 'Finding Scotland's Allotments', 2007. Go to: www.sags.org.uk

40 Glasgow Council minute Vol. C1 3.64, November 1920 – April 1921, p. 296.

41 Email from Sarah Robinson, ng2.

42 Email from Linda Pike, vice chair Glasgow Allotments Forum.

43 Email from Mark Thirgood, member Scottish Allotments and Gardens Society.

44 Margaret Campbell http://www.transitiontownwestkirby.org.uk/ files/allotment_waiting_lists_scotland_2010.xls

45 See responses to the Community Empowerment Bill consultation www.scotland.gov.uk/Publications/2013/02/4397 www.scotland.gov.uk/Publications/2014/02/2073

46 Email from Sandy Paterson, Glasgow City Council.

47 Quoted in www.sags.org.uk/docs/.../CBEPostConference Papers.pdf

48 See www.sags.org.uk/docs/Responses/CERB/Chap6 Response.pdf

49 *Daily Record*, June 01, 2012.

50 Email from Ailsa Jackson, Scottish Government.

51 Email from Stuart MacKenzie, Inverleith Allotments.

52 Linda Pike, as above.

53 Go to: www.glasgowallotmentsforum.org.uk

54 Go to: http://www.earthcharterinaction.org/content/pages/ Read-the-Charter.html

55 Caitlin O'Brian DeSilvey, 'To all the Ingenious Allotment Gardeners in Scotland', *op.cit.*

56 Scottish Allotments newsletter 2012.

57 See Edinburgh Council's Allotment Strategy:

www.edinburgh.gov.uk/download/.../allotment_strategy_2
010-15

58 This can be accessed at: http://www.sags.org.uk/docs/
Scotland AllotmentDesignGuide.pdf

59 Peter Wright article given to the authors.

60 Linda Pike, as above.

61 Quoted in the minutes of the Dundee Allotment Strategy
Implementation Group.

62 For information go to: http://permacultureprinciples.com/

63 This document can be viewed at: http://www.unep.org/
Documents.Multilingual/Default.asp?documentid=97&arti
cleid=1503

64 David Crouch and Colin Ward, *The Allotment: Its
Landscape and Culture*, Mushroom Bookshop,
Nottingham, 1994.

65 Taken from DAC & Cities web pages: www.dac.dk/en/dac-
cities/sustainable-cities/all-cases/green-city/aarhus-
allotments-more-popular-than-ever/

66 Private communication with Lesley Riddoch.

67 *Boston Natural Areas Network 2003*. Web page no longer
available.

68 Asian Community Development Corporation Boston 2003.
Web page no longer available.

69 See 'Urban Agriculture Notes' on 'Havana's Popular
Gardens: Sustainable Urban Agriculture at
http://www.cityfarmer.org/cuba.html

70 Crouch Ward, *op.cit.*

71 Department for Communities and Local Government,
Allotments disposal guidance: Safeguards and alternatives,
2014.

72 Crouch and Ward, *op cit.*, p. 257.

73 Linda Pike, as above.

74 Sandy Paterson, as above.

Useful reports and documents

1 Scottish Allotments and Gardens Society Publications are available for download at www.sags.org.uk:

   Growing Scotland 2007
   Finding Scotland's Allotments 2007
   Allotments – a Scottish Plotholder's Guide
   Scotland's Allotment Site Design Guide 2013

2 Heritage of Glasgow's Allotments report is available for download at www.gah.org.uk

3 Current (2014) consultations and legislation affecting allotments –

   Consultations on Community Empowerment Bill
   National Planning Framework and Scottish Planning Policy
   Delivery of Regeneration in Scotland Inquiry
   Land reform

Additional information

You can find more information related to this book by visiting the *Raising Spirits* section of the Postcards from Scotland website – www.postcardsfromscotland.co.uk

Book Series from Argyll Publishing and the Centre for Confidence and Wellbeing

This series of short books is designed to stimulate and communicate new thinking and ways of living. The first volumes appeared in late 2012 priced £5.99.

Series editor and advisory group: Carol Craig of the Centre for Confidence and Wellbeing is the series editor. She is supported by a small advisory group comprising Fred Shedden, Chair of the Centre's Board, Professor Phil Hanlon and Jean Urquhart MSP.

Title:	**Scotland's Local Food Revolution**
Author:	Mike Small
ISBN:	978 1 908931 26 9

Title:	**After Now – What next for a healthy Scotland?**
Authors:	Phil Hanlon and Sandra Carlisle
ISBN:	978 1 908931 05 4

Title:	**The Great Takeover – How materialism, the media and markets now dominate our lives**
Author:	Carol Craig
ISBN:	978 1 908931 06 1

Title:	**The New Road – Charting Scotland's inspirational communities**
Authors:	Alf Young and Ewan Young
ISBN:	978 1 908931 07 8

Title:	**Letting Go– Breathing new life into organisations**
Authors:	Tony Miller and Gordon Hall
ISBN:	978 1 908931 49 8

Also published as **e**-books